THE SOCIAL CLIMBER'S BIBLE

THE SOCIAL CLIMBER'S BIBLE

A Book of Manners, Practical Tips,
and Spiritual Advice for the Upwardly Mobile

DIRK WITTENBORN
and JAZZ JOHNSON

PENGUIN BOOKS

PENGUIN BOOKS

Published by the Penguin Group
Penguin Group (USA) LLC
375 Hudson Street
New York, New York 10014

USA | Canada | UK | Ireland | Australia | New Zealand | India | South Africa | China
penguin.com
A Penguin Random House Company

First published in Penguin Books 2014

Library of Congress Cataloging-in-Publication Data

Wittenborn, Dirk, author.
The social climber's bible : a book of manners, practical tips, and spiritual advice for the
upwardly mobile / Dirk Wittenborn, Jazz Johnson.
pages cm
ISBN 978-0-14-312520-4 (hardback)
1. Etiquette.   2. Social mobility.   I. Johnson, Jazz, author.   II. Title.
BJ1853.W58 2014
158.2—dc23
2014012089

Printed in the United States of America
1   3   5   7   9   10   8   6   4   2

Set in Adobe Garamond
Designed by Spring Hoteling

CONTENTS

FOREWORD

irk Wittenborn and his niece Jazz Johnson have seen the
best and worst social climbers of our age at work, watched
them succeed and fail in their assault on the summits of
high society, new money, old money, show business, downtown,
uptown, New York, Los Angeles, Europe, and beyond: Between
them, they have spent more than fifty years marveling at the
skills, ambition, and nerve of those who have the moral fortitude
to go for the gold. In the course of their research on climbing,
the authors also made a startling personal discovery that has affected their own life's journey: Social climbers were not only getting ahead of them, they were also having more fun. Their
groundbreaking self-help manual, *The Social Climber's Bible*, offers two very different but uniquely revealing perspectives on upward mobility.

Ms. Johnson is a thirty-six-year-old Johnson & Johnson
heiress. A former debutante and graduate of Barnard College,
she has been photographed for *Vogue* and has created a line of
her own jewelry. A distinguished horsewoman, Ms. Johnson has

won in the American Hunter division at many top horse shows in the country. She manages her family estate, serves on Johnson & Johnson's board of charitable foundations, is master of the Essex Fox Hounds, and has named her four dogs after alcoholic beverages. Jazz is an insider in that rarefied world fans of *Gossip Girl* and *Downton Abbey* dream about and social climbers of all ages want to belong to.

Her fascination with the subject of Mountaineering was sparked at age seven when she asked her parents why her dashing billionaire grandfather, J. Seward Johnson Sr., former vice president of J & J, world-renowned yachtsman, philanthropist, and founder of the Harbor Branch Oceanographic Institute, was no longer married to her elegant and sophisticated Bostonian grandmother. The answer: Grandpa had met and married an incredibly gifted social climber who, besides being a penniless Polish immigrant forty-one years Grandpa's junior, also happened to be the upstairs maid.

Dirk Wittenborn, a novelist and screenwriter, is a producer of the Emmy-nominated HBO documentary *Born Rich*. His fiction has often explored the interplay of class and money in the American dream. Early in his career via a brief connection to *Saturday Night Live*, the highlight of which was being filmed teaching cats to swim, he picked up enough bad habits and celebrity friends to become a part of New York City's downtown demimonde. It was edifying to Wittenborn to watch how quickly some of Gotham's most prominent young social climbers befriended him in the mistaken belief that he might know someone who could help them; even more enlightening was observing the grace with which those disappointed Mountaineers quickly dropped him. Old enough to remember when sex was safe and cocaine wasn't addictive, Mr. Wittenborn was on the scene to witness that seminal moment in American history when, as he says, "ass-kissing became networking."

In short, whereas Ms. Johnson belongs to the most exclusive clubs in the world, Mr. Wittenborn has been kicked out of them. Like those pioneering sex researchers of the sixties and seventies, Masters and Johnson, who dared to show the world that sex was nothing to be ashamed of, Wittenborn and Johnson have dared to offer an unbiased exploration of our present-day culture's final taboo, the last form of social intercourse the world still refuses to be candid about—social climbing.

INTRODUCTION

E very year the self-help industry inundates us with new books, blogs, and TV gurus offering advice about how to maximize your human potential with promises of surefire steps guaranteed to turn your life around—sadly, those steps rarely lead you anywhere except to the depressing thought that you are the person you are, have the life you have, because that is all you deserve. That is, until now!

We have written this book because none of these guides to a brighter future has the honesty or common sense to mention—much less recommend—what scientific research, our personal experience, and interviews with highly accomplished people in all walks of life have shown us to be inarguably true.

> The surest, fastest, and most painless method of improving your position in this highly competitive world and giving yourself a chance to step into the winners circle is . . . SOCIAL CLIMBING.

Now, we know what you're thinking. You hate social climbers. Right? That's what everybody says. But before dismissing our offer to change your life, ask yourself this one simple question: Would you cancel meeting up with your mother, sister, old friend from college, boyfriend, girlfriend, spouse, child, or that nice old lady with the wooden leg who lives down the hall with her cats if you were invited to hang out with: Bono? Michelle Obama? George Clooney, Bill Gates, Kate Moss, Beyoncé, the Pope, Derek Jeter, Lady Gaga, the Dalai Lama, Damien Hirst, David Bowie, Jerry Seinfeld, Prince William, or the Duchess of Cambridge? Sean "Diddy" Combs, Germany's Chancellor Angela Merkel, Gérard Depardieu, Roger Federer, Stephen Hawking . . . ? Someone whose friendship could enrich your life and at the very least give you an experience to make your friends envious?

If your answer's "No," you're lying.

If your answer's "Yes," your qualms about becoming a social climber are irrelevant, because you already are one. We're not telling you what to want, just how to get it.

Are you brave enough to be honest about what you really desire? Willing to listen to what your inner child tells you you're entitled to? Do you have the courage to open your eyes to the importance of the superficial in postmodern life? If so, you already have the makings of a good social climber. And our book will make you a great one!

Follow our instructions, embrace our dos and don'ts of upward mobility, and social climbing will cease to be something you have to do in order to get ahead and instead become a way of life—a shining path as contemplative and revealing of the life force within you as Buddhism, only a hell of a lot more fun.

How It All Began

According to anthropologists, social climbing was imprinted on human behavior before primitive man descended from the trees. If you didn't have it in you to be the alpha male or female, the second best way to ensure your survival was to develop the social skills that would enable you to become the new best friend of those with the sharpest teeth and the most lethal hunting skills, before they decided to eat you. Like the ability to make a flint hand ax, or start a fire by rubbing two sticks together, social climbing was both a tool and a skill that could not only radically improve the quality of life for those who walked on their hind legs, it could save your life.

EMPOWERING THOUGHT #1

Throughout our evolution, from Cro-Magnon through Neanderthal to Homo sapiens, how to make friends and influence humanoids has been a cornerstone of civilization, or, as a theologian might put it: Social climbing is God's way of leveling the playing field.

How Did Social Climbing Get Such a Bad Reputation?

Think of all the varieties of intimate human behavior and interaction that were once unfairly judged by the so-called moral authorities to be bad, unhealthy, and, worse, unnatural that are now embraced as varieties of normal. To nineteenth-century Victorians, masturbation, premarital fornication, oral sex, sodomy, and homosexuality were vices. Today, even the Archbishop of Canterbury recognizes them as beautiful manifestations of the drives that make us human. So why does a human form of social intercourse as age-old, widespread, and instinctual as social climbing remain a stigma?

Consider the fate of two of the most famous fictional characters of the twentieth century. In F. Scott Fitzgerald's *The Great Gatsby*, the über–upwardly mobile Jay Gatsby isn't just punished, he's shot in his swimming pool for a murder he didn't commit. And how about poor Eve Harrington in *All About Eve*—she pays doubly for her climbing ways. Not only is she blackmailed by the slimy theater critic portrayed by George Sanders, but once she makes it to the big time, she has to pay off by sleeping with him.

> How is it our culture can forgive banks their debts, the Kardashians their toxic bad taste, and Donald Trump his hair but still discriminate against the social climber?

Psychologists tell us that a healthy friendship is based on common interests, hobbies, values. If you never get the chance to socialize with your boss, or better yet, the president of the company you work for, how are you ever going to know whether you have the same interests and values? Yes, you are in the same income bracket as the drone in the cubicle next to you, but isn't it a perverse and reverse bigotry to assume that just because the CEO has three more zeros at the end of his paycheck than you do, he is unworthy of your making an effort to get to know him?

Know that social climbing is an expression invented by snobs to make other snobs feel superior to you. Dictionary definitions of social climbing as the pursuit of friendships with those of a higher social status assume and perpetuate a notion we think is offensive, i.e., that one group of people is superior to another. We believe you are not only as good as anybody else, you're *better*. Because you, by reading *The Social Climber's Bible*, have joined us in our fight to redefine social climbing, to establish it as a positive attribute rather than a pejorative designed to shame you into believing you are not good enough to go to the party.

Social climbing is not about getting to know people because you want something. It is about giving highly successful people a chance to get to know you well enough to realize you're a great person, a special person, a person worth their friendship. And if they help you when you're in need, well, isn't that what real friendship's all about?

We don't teach our children to search out playmates who will do bad things to them. Yet as adults, we are made to feel ashamed for seeking friendships that can help us fulfill our dreams. And turning dreams into reality is what *The Social Climber's Bible* is all about.

Freedom from the tyranny of the class system, the opportunity for upward mobility, was the dream that brought the immigrant to America. Europe's peasants came to our shores to escape the unfairness of the feudal system they were born into, to have their God-given right to climb the ladder.

EMPOWERING THOUGHT #2

Given that the "pursuit of happiness" is guaranteed in the Declaration of Independence, and that upward mobility is a key ingredient in the melting pot that made our country great, social climbing is as American as apple pie.

So, if social climbing is democracy in action, why all the ugly pseudonyms: ASSLICKER, BROWNNOSER, SUCK-UP?

Of course, one's tongue and/or the exchange of bodily fluids are often involved in social climbing, but for now let's concentrate on how social climbing became a pejorative.

The demonization of the social climber began with the Puritans. Faced with a harsh winter and failed crops, our Pilgrim forefathers would have starved to death had they not shamelessly sucked up to the Indians and invited them to cater that first Thanksgiving. Conversely, if the Indians had had a problem with social climbers, they would have butchered the newcomers when they first showed up at Plymouth Rock. The original sin and seeds of hypocrisy surrounding the stigmatization of "social climbing" can be found in the Pilgrims' behavior at subsequent Thanksgivings. As soon as the Pilgrims had enough food to feed themselves, the Indians were disinvited to the party. Worse, our forefathers thanked their aboriginal hosts who saved them from starvation by proceeding to steal their land, infect them with syphilis, and kill off those who refused to die a natural death.

These early American asslickers then went to work ingratiating themselves with those who commanded the next rung on the ladder—the English Crown's governors, generals, magistrates, and tax collectors. And once the Puritans had used them to get rich enough to establish their own ruling class, they thanked the royals by starting a revolution and disinviting them to the party. Having gotten more than their fair share of the pie by befriending and then betraying any and all who helped them climb to the top, our pioneer American aristocracy had no intention of letting the succeeding generations of immigrants who followed them to America exploit them in similar fashion. The Puritans didn't just torch witches; they tried to burn the ladder.

The rich have always known the value of social climbing. The nineteenth-century nouveau riche made few friends on the way up. But once they had made too much money to be snubbed, they solidified their position by marrying themselves or their offspring into families who, though not as rich, had cachet, class, accomplishment, and connections that wealth alone could not buy; or at least, not unless they had an awful lot of money.

Railroad robber baron Cornelius Vanderbilt gave his daughter's hand in marriage to the comparatively impoverished but supremely well-connected Duke of Marlborough and in doing so, was finally able to snub the Astors. So it goes a hundred years later. Ralph Lifshitz changes his surname to Lauren, makes billions selling the preppie look to people who didn't go to prep school, has a son who marries Lauren Bush, the granddaughter of George H. W. Bush and the niece of George W. Bush, who demographics alone would lead one to believe will be the last two WASP presidents of the United States. We mention this not in any way to imply Ralph was obsessed with or fetishized the glamour of snobbery, or that Lauren + Lauren is not a love match, but merely to underscore the point that social climbing is not just about money. It's about having the taste and intelligence to ignore what less ambitious souls have told you since you were a child you can't have and shouldn't want . . . and having it all.

Take a lesson from the Middleton sisters: Set your priorities and put yourself in a petri dish where great things will happen to you and the sky's the limit. Did Kate and Pippa stop climbing when they were nicknamed the Wisteria Sisters in honor of that clingy, climbing, flowering vine? Of course not; they climbed faster. Kate went from daughter of a "trolley-dolly," aka an airline stewardess, to mother of the future king of England. How Pippa will top that remains to be seen, but we know she won't settle for second best, unless his name is Prince Harry.

Who are those boldfaced names chiseled on the walls of art museums, opera houses, hospitals, and Ivy League universities? They're social climbers. If you pay for the new wing to a cultural institution, you are no longer a crass, pushy vampire squid who beat the rap on insider trading, you are the new best friend to the cultural elite of the world. Though *Roget's Thesaurus* would disagree, philanthropy is now and has always been a synonym for social climbing.

The rich don't make six-figure donations to get their children into the right nursery school because they like the teachers. They want to make sure their children start learning the secrets of social climbing by the time they're toilet-trained—secrets they don't want you to know, secrets that give them an unfair advantage, but secrets *The Social Climber's Bible* believes you have a right to know.

EMPOWERING THOUGHT #3
You are a special person who could be more special if you had more special friends.

Whether you dream of partying with billionaires or running for political office, or long for a job that won't require you to ever have to ask anyone again, "Do you want fries with that order?" or simply want to know what it's like to knock back a six-pack with the reality stars of *Duck Dynasty*, we can show you a shortcut to the top. However, before we start, a few words of caution:

**WARNING: DO NOT READ
THIS BOOK IN PUBLIC**
Though social climbing has a long and admirable tradition, and has played as significant a role in our human evolution as our opposable thumbs,

it is best not to advertise your decision to master the art of social climbing. Put your copy of *The Social Climber's Bible* in the same drawer where you hide your porno and sex aids. If it is discovered by a snoopy friend or family member, swear on the life of a loved one it belongs to someone else.

THE SOCIAL CLIMBER'S BIBLE

WHY YOU HAVE WHAT IT TAKES,
EVEN IF YOU DON'T

Life teaches us that the less you have to bring to the party in terms of looks, charm, education, professional achievement, intelligence, worldly experience, famous relatives, and yes, of course, that ultimate game changer, money—the harder it will be for you to get to the top. That is, unless you're a Mountaineer.

Though the world is neither fair nor democratic, those lacking any or all of the above assets will be happy to know that if you are mediocre-looking and lacking in special skills, you have an advantage when it comes to a career in climbing. Why? Because the more accomplished and attractive you are, the more likely it is you will be pegged as a social climber.

What separates the good social climber (that is, the invisible one) from the bad (i.e., the obvious) has nothing to do with how pushy, self-serving, or ruthless you are. It's all about manners. And we will teach you tricks of etiquette that will make your climb seem as innocent and uncalculated as a child's smile.

Proper etiquette for the social climber involves far more than just remembering to say please and thank you. Social climbing is a strategy for getting more out of life. As such, bluffs, feints, tactical retreats, flanking maneuvers, ambushes, forced marches, and yes, unfortunately, collateral damage to innocents are involved in victory.

If done correctly, it is not unlike cyber warfare. You are the virus, and the enemy—all those who have access to things you want who are not yet your new best friends—will have no idea they're under attack until you have gained entrée and moved on to the next party.

But before we decide which stratagems will work best for you, let's begin by asking ourselves a few personal questions:

What Are My Assets?

Not sure? Why don't we start by removing our clothes (that includes underwear) and taking a good hard look at ourselves in the mirror.

If you don't like what you see, remember: Penicillin started out as mold.

Would you describe yourself as less than gorgeous? Subhandsome? Are you overweight? Out of shape? Plagued by the heartbreak of psoriasis? Would you refuse to have sex with someone who resembled yourself?

EMPOWERING THOUGHT #4

We are not like all the other self-help books
that tell you to love yourself just as you are, not

> as the world tells you you should be and then
> proceed to make you feel bad for not going to
> the gym, and/or for drinking alone, and/or
> for self-medicating with prescription drugs. We
> want you to appreciate your shortcomings as
> much as we do.

So now that you're naked, we want you to repeat our Mantra for Upward Mobility. I CARE ENOUGH ABOUT ME NOT TO BELIEVE ANYTHING THEY SAY ABOUT ME IS TRUE IF I DON'T WANT IT TO BE. I WILL NOT BE JUDGED.

As you're repeating your new mantra, here's another thought that will cheer you up: One of the great things about social climbing is that being a beautiful person, either physically or spiritually, is not always an asset.

Particularly as you climb to the higher rungs of the ladder, you will discover that those worth getting to know—the megarich, the hugely powerful, what we like to call Whales—are extraordinary people but rarely extraordinarily physically attractive people.

If we were being mean we might say Microsoft's Paul Allen has the look of a mortician and Bill Gates resembles a snail out of his shell; or suggest corporate raider Ron Perelman was the inspiration for SpongeBob's snobby neighbor, Squidward. Our point is, if you check the *Forbes* 400, the top of the food chain isn't pretty. Movie stars, supermodels, and rock stars may be better-looking, but they're ugly in their own way. Human nature being what it is, people who are filthy rich and powerful and famous and less than beautiful want to surround themselves with people who will make them feel more attractive by comparison, i.e., you.

The privileged elite, the Mountaineers' portals to a brighter future, are what we call Big Fish. Though we can be accused of mixing metaphors, you will soon discover that one can't get close to the top of the mountain without learning how to recognize, hook, and filet Big Fish. Having spent their lives working and climbing to get where they are, Big Fish want friends they can count on to envy them, friends who will make them feel superior: friends like you.

Those readers whose assets do not include physical beauty should also know they have one huge advantage when it comes to social climbing. If you are clearly more attractive than the Big Fish, i.e., gorgeous/handsome, they will want to have sex with you. If you have sex with them, they will either be disappointed or, worse, fall for you and want to have sex with you again and again and again, thereby becoming possessive and limiting your ability to move on and seduce one of their richer and more powerful friends.

Now, stop chanting. Put your clothes back on, and let's take a look in your closet.

As Coco Chanel said, dress as you wish to be perceived. First and foremost, social climbers should look like they belong . . . anywhere. Unless, of course, it's in your interest to look like you don't belong, which is a more complex strategy that will be covered later. You want to fit in and at the same time set yourself apart just enough so that you'll be remembered. Your outfit should tell a story—invite conversation, curiosity, and just enough envy to make people think you're worthy of their friendship.

A large hat with a veil for women, or a fedora for men, pulled rakishly low over one eye, can make the difference between being remembered as the guest with the unfortunate nose and being recalled as the fun person in the chapeau.

As a rule of thumb, never be overdressed, for the simple reason that it will make it clear how hard you're trying to be something you're not. Those who actually belong to whatever social strata you're trying to move up into won't be trying hard. Which means no matter how hard you're working at pretending to be someone other than yourself, it should appear at all times that you are just being yourself.

Of course, occasionally arriving in a ball gown or a tuxedo to a casual event can work wonders for you if you wear it in a way that implies you're on your way to somewhere fancier, better, and more socially promising, which in turn will give your hosts, who more often than not are as socially ambitious as yourself, the false impression that you might have connections they can exploit to their advantage.

Here are some suggested fun looks for the social climber—looks that will make you seem worth getting to know at a glance but not strange. A word to the wise: You want your outfit to be a conversation starter, not a joke.

If you're a Sikh, go with the turban and uncut hair, aka the *kes*, along with the other four Ks, the *kanga* (wooden comb), *kara* (steel or iron bracelet), *kirpan* (dagger), and the special sexy *kachhera* (underwear). Look what the Mormon Church's magical briefs did for Mitt Romney. If you have a drop of Scottish blood in you, wear your kilt and sporran when flambéing the boulevard. Indonesian (or just look it), a blue blazer and a sarong is a worldly ice breaker. For those who are from the Arabian Gulf states, a word to the wise: Though a head scarf is dashing, a burka and full robes might get in the way of your dance floor fun, unless of course you're the daughter of an Emirate emir and have a disco in your 747.

Whatever look you go for, stick with it—not having to waste time shopping or deciding what to wear will give you more time to work on your social life.

How to Sound Like a Somebody

The rules have changed since *My Fair Lady*'s Eliza Doolittle had to learn how to talk fancy. The era when an accent could hinder your climb is fortunately behind us. Sounding as if you come from somewhere when you come from nowhere can be a plus. Texas twang, southern drawl, English, Australian, Pakistani, whatever, don't lose it, go with it. It will make you seem more authentic. The one caveat to this rule, of course, is if your accent is "Jersey Shore"—in this case, if elocution lessons are not an option, the quickest way for you to get respect is to let your host or hostess know that your family is in organized crime.

In terms of presentation, one last piece of advice: A good social climber doesn't look or smell nervous. If you belong, you don't sweat. Now because you're soon going to be stepping into situations where you don't belong, carry a clean handkerchief and a good deodorant on your person at all times. Never forget: When a social climber steps into a room, he or she should smell like a breath of fresh air.

DOES BEING A SOCIAL CLIMBER MEAN
I HAVE TO BECOME A PHONY?

Telling people they look gorgeous when in fact they're an eyesore or praising them for being wise when they have the intelligence of a cocker spaniel doesn't make you a phony, it makes you a kind person.

> The good social climber knows that the truth is often hurtful, cruel, and, most important, does not make you popular.

If you have qualms about telling the white lies, whoppers, exaggerations, and confabulations of fact and fiction that will not only make your climb go easier and faster but also make people like you more, consider this:

Both scientists and philosophers agree that no truth is absolute, all truths are subjective, and reality is a matter of perception. That is, what small minds might call a lie is not. Social climbers should think like legendary quantum physicist Hugh Everett, who said, among other things, that anything that can happen, does happen in some universe somewhere.

For example, say you're a man who has been invited to a social function where you're expected to wear a suit and tie and you have nothing in your closet except track suits, hoodies, and sweats. If you show up and admit to your host or hostess that you are dressed for a game of b-ball because you don't own a suit, your chances of making a successful impression are far slimmer than if you arrive in your athletic gear and apologize for the way you are underdressed by explaining that you were just shooting hoops over at the Nets new arena in Brooklyn with Jay Z.

Could it be true? In a physicist's theoretical parallel universe it could!

Does the white lie make you seem like the kind of person your host will want to show off to his even better-connected friends—most definitely!

The only question the social climber should ask when employing the physicists' and philosophers' creative approach to reality is simply—WILL I GET CAUGHT?

In this case, if your host is white and has a net worth under a hundred million dollars, the odds of his bumping into Jay Z and finding out you're lying are longer than the odds of your being struck by a meteor while sitting on the couch watching the Nets play on television.

EMPOWERING THOUGHT #5

For the social climber, honesty is rarely the best policy.

You must always remember that those who have far more money, power, and access than you do will undoubtedly have been climbing for years and are far more experienced Mountaineers than you are. As such, they will have a built-in bullshit detector.

Simply saying everything and everybody is fabulous won't make the Big Fish think you're especially remarkable, especially if they're French. The key to keeping your betters' bullshit detector from going off and avoiding being written off as an obvious suck-up or straightforward sycophant requires three things: 1) patience, 2) planning, and 3) polishing reality, that is, a willingness to confabulate one or more small white lies that will make someone other than yourself look and feel good.

Here's how it works: First demonstrate yourself to be a critical-thinking person of discerning taste by subtly putting down those you are sure the Big Fish thinks are either above or beneath him (this should be done in private to make sure that a third party doesn't quote you and thus prevent you from becoming friends at a later date with those you have dissed to ingratiate yourself).

Having established a bond of shared disdain, retreat.

Whether you wait a week or an hour to sink your hook depends on your circumstances and the amount of alcohol and/or drugs the Big Fish has consumed. The important thing to remember is you should wait until the Big Fish is feeling good, happy, and relaxed, surrounded by friends. Then, at a suitable lull in the conversation, interject, "You know, Barbara (or whatever name your Big Fish goes by), the last time we talked you said the most brilliant thing about [art, the junk bond market, romance, parenting, whatever]."

Now even though the brilliant statement you just referred to was never made by Barbara, and even if she has in fact never made a brilliant statement in her life, when you proceed to attribute a brilliant statement to her that she never made, she, and everybody else, is going to be impressed.

Offer up a reworked truism of Oscar Wilde's, plagiarize Fran Lebowitz, or paraphrase Jon Stewart on *The Daily Show*. For instance, if you were talking about art, you might want to endow the Big Fish with these words of wisdom. "Great art doesn't idealize the real, it realizes the ideal."

The Big Fish isn't going to say, "I never said such a clever thing in my life." He is going to smile, swallow it hook, line, and sinker, and take credit for the words of wisdom you invented for him.

More important for you, that Big Fish is immediately going to think two things: a) Sometimes I forget how smart I am, and b) *you* are an intelligent and discerning judge of character and must be invited back to remind him of other clever things he's forgotten he said.

EMPOWERING THOUGHT #6

It is rare to encounter an individual who will think you are stupid for saying that he or she is the most intelligent person in the room, but such individuals do exist, particularly in the financial world; think of Bernie Madoff.

Social climbers do not improvise on reality—telling white lies that make other people feel good about themselves—because they don't know the difference between fact and fiction. Social climbers are simply realists; they take the world as it is and try to change it by improving their own position in it. Take comfort in the fact that the twenty-first century is the golden age of misinformation. One only has to listen to Fox News to know there is no such thing as hard fact. Besides, you are lying for a good cause—*you*.

Men and women we admire, candidates for the highest office in the land, take liberties with reality every day. If former president George W. Bush can make up words like "misunderestimate," if former secretary of state Hillary Clinton can tell a whopper about running from enemy gunfire at an airbase in Bosnia when she in fact was caught on video with a bunch of schoolgirls presenting her with bouquets, if Mitt Romney can quote imaginary statistics to support an economic plan designed to make him and his Big Fish friends richer and you poorer, why shouldn't hardworking social climbers be allowed to take a few liberties in advancing themselves?

Not just to pick on politicians, what about all the actors and actresses who swear they never had a face-lift but have fewer wrinkles at fifty than they did at twenty-five? Like margarines that insist they taste just like butter, people, especially professional personalities who market themselves as a brand, are rarely all they claim to be. And why should they be? False advertising is a great American tradition.

Though you are still several steps away from beginning your ascent in public, it's important for you to have a practical understanding of how your ability to improvise and improve your backstory can be helpful.

Imagine you're at a party. It's in a mansion in Beverly Hills and Adam Levine and David Bowie have just sung an impromptu duet. Uniformed waiters pass hors d'oeuvres, silver trays laden with bite-size delectables—truffled quail eggs, crab tostadas, baby potatoes overflowing with Beluga caviar; this is the kind of party you'll be going to three or four evenings a week if you master the lessons of this book.

Now imagine you find yourself on the edge of a group of people whom you don't know but recognize as being more prosperous, connected, and attractive than yourself. What's more, they are enjoying drawing attention to the social gulf between your life and theirs by nattering on about, say, what a fantastic time they all had on their various safaris in Africa. As they compare the amenities offered by Abercrombie & Kent versus those provided by Eco Tours Unlimited, you, having never set foot in Africa, feel understandably left out. If you have always wanted to go on safari but can't afford a ticket to Buffalo, much less Nairobi, you're going to feel doubly left out.

If you interject yourself into this conversation with the truth and say, "Gee, I always wanted to go to Africa, but I can't afford it," you will not only succeed in making the group feel guilty for being richer and more worldly than you, you will also make yourself feel like even more of an outsider. However, if you volunteer a vague "Africa has always been a magical place for me," the group will assume not only that you have been to Africa, but that you might have had a more spiritual experience there than they were able to purchase. Suddenly, you will belong. It will be a wonderful feeling, like Christmas and Chanukah combined but better.

If someone asks for the details of this trip you never made, what safari company you booked or which hotel you stayed in, answer honestly, "I don't remember." Then quickly and convincingly add, "I was only seven when my grandmother took me on safari." Having a grandmother who takes you on safari as a child will not only give your act provenance, it will also give you the kind of exotic patina of a privileged past that's invaluable to the climber. Plus, if people can't place you, they can't put you down.

If people in the group have known you for several months, do not worry about their wondering why you never mentioned this nonexistent globe-trotting granny before. They will simply assume that you remained silent on the subject of Africa and your granny for so long because you, unlike them, are not a show-off.

Whether you want to merely stretch the truth when you begin your adventures in Mountaineering or confabulate a whole new you is something every social climber has to decide for themselves. But if you are going to invent more than one or two fictional relatives to make yourself more interesting to strangers, it's best to write down their names and keep a record of what you claim to have done with them over the years.

A word of caution regarding reinvention. Claiming to have gone to Harvard when you in fact flunked out of community college is asking for trouble in the age of the Internet. Likewise, claiming to be a Rockefeller is risky. Besides the fact that the last two people who tried it are currently serving time, even if you legally change your name, avoid running into a real Rockefeller, and stay on the right side of the law, you will be expected to pick up the tab and be inundated with business proposals and requests for loans that you will be unable to refuse without seeming cheap.

How to Name-Drop the Dead

One of the safest ways to make it seem that you've lived a far more exciting life than you have is to casually claim friendship with a genuinely famous, rich, and or/powerful person who is no longer alive.

Offhandedly mention any of the following and people will treat you differently:

"Leonard Bernstein taught me to play 'Chopsticks.'"

"When my mom dated Jimi Hendrix, Janis Joplin used to babysit for me."

"David Foster Wallace and I roomed together at the psychiatric hospital."

"Heath Ledger and I bicycled across Tasmania."

"James Gandolfini taught me how to make lobster fra diavolo."

Acquire an eight-by-ten glossy of the dead somebody you're claiming to have been close personal friends with, write a touching personal inscription to yourself, sign the person's name, and hang it on a discreet wall of your home, a place where your guests will be sure to see it but not so prominently placed so it will seem like you're trying to impress.

For any readers who are still worried that there's something "phony" about social climbing, or are having a last-minute attack of conscience in regard to taking liberties with the truth—that is, misrepresenting themselves to a Big Fish—ask yourself: If we are all equal, how is it some people actually do get to play "Chopsticks" with Leonard Bernstein, or go on safari with their grandmother, or meet Heath Ledger before he got famous and died?

Is it right or fair that the man or woman who's CEO of the company you work for and can change your life makes a thousand times more per hour than you do? Are Big Fish really that much smarter and more talented than the rest of us, or are they just lucky? Or simply more ruthless?

> Social climbing is class warfare. You are not deceiving people like yourselves, you're infiltrating behind enemy lines, taking on the powers that be, the powers that have prospered at your expense and tried to keep the secrets of social climbing from you.

Know that if you follow the tenets laid out in *The Social Climber's Bible*, when you get to the top, you, unlike those whose friendship you'll need to complete your quest, will deserve to be there.

3

THE WITTENBORN-JOHNSON PSYCHOLOGICAL APTITUDE TEST FOR SOCIAL CLIMBERS

Our research has shown that from a psychological standpoint, social climbers fall into six basic personality types. Knowing from the start what kind of climber you inherently are will make a huge difference when it comes to how far, fast, and high you climb. When taking the following psychological test, we urge you to be honest. Know that we are not judging you or trying to pigeonhole you. Rather, our hope is to maximize your human potential by helping you identify attributes in yourself that smaller minds might call flaws.

a Tactician many therapists regard as nothing more than a sociopath who likes to party. Note: Those of you who are currently on prescribed psychoactive medication or are self-medicating with nonprescription drugs, please take your meds far enough in advance of taking this test to give yourself an accurate sense of who you are when you're fucked-up.

1. You are swimming in a fabulous swimming pool that belongs to someone else. You suddenly feel the urge to urinate. Do you:

    a.   Get out of the pool and find a bathroom.

    b.   Pee in the pool and hope there are no chemicals in the water that will reveal your offense.

    c.   Deliberately pee in the pool because those in the pool with you have not invited you to their parties.

    d.   Pee in the pool because you think others should consider themselves lucky to be in the same pool with you and your pee.

    e.   Pee in the pool because you are so drunk and/or old you do not know you are peeing.

    f.   Pee in the pool and blame it on someone else.

2. The last time you slept with your best friend's boyfriend/girlfriend/husband/wife, you did so because:

    a.   You have already slept with their parents and figure why not make it a family affair.

    b.   You suffer from low self-esteem, and you are running out of exciting things to discuss with your therapist.

    c.   You are jealous that your best friend is more successful and attractive than you are.

    d.   Your best friend boasted that their boyfriend/girlfriend/husband/wife was better in bed than you.

    e.   You had dosed them with Ecstasy.

    f.   Your best friend's boyfriend/girlfriend/husband/wife was so cool, you hoped having sex with them would make you cool.

3. When you took your SATs in high school, you cheated because:

    a.   You recognize cheating and getting away with it is a valuable life skill.

    b.   You honestly believe that you deserve an unfair advantage.

c. You knew you needed to get into a good college if you wanted to get a job in the financial services industry that would allow you to cheat people out of large sums of money.

d. SAT tests don't reflect what truly distinguishes one human being from another . . . like, duh, being popular.

e. You come from a country where cheating has a long and honorable place in the culture.

f. You know you're not as smart as you bullied people into believing you are.

4. When a young, handsome/beautiful, talented celebrity dies from a drug overdose you feel:

a. Sad because you will never get a chance to meet them and become friends with them.

b. Sad because you are sad when anyone dies.

c. Jealous because the celebrity is still getting more attention than you are even though they are dead.

d. Compelled to point out that the dead celebrity was not as handsome/beautiful/talented as everybody said.

e. Relieved because no one will be able to prove you have been lying about having an affair with the celebrity when you were in rehab.

f. Happy because there is one less person in the universe for you to envy.

5. Imagine you are stranded on a desert island with your boss, boyfriend/girlfriend/spouse, Scarlett Johansson, Channing Tatum, and the admissions director at Princeton. Who would you eat first?

a. Your boyfriend/girlfriend/spouse, because with them gone you might get the chance to have a *Blue Lagoon* moment with Scarlett and/or Channing.

b. Scarlett or Channing, because if you don't your boyfriend/girlfriend/spouse will definitely have a *Blue Lagoon* moment with one or both of them.

b. Your boss, because if you survive and he gets eaten, you'll have a shot at his job.

c. Scarlett Johansson, because she looks tasty, and you can be relatively confident she is gluten-free.

d. Scarlett and/or Tatum, because you are tired of hearing them talk about how hard it is to be famous.

e. The Princeton admissions director, be-cause you didn't get into Princeton.

6. You don't feel guilty reading your best friend's secret diary without permission because:

 a. You know that knowledge is power.

 b. You already know they think bad things about you, and it doesn't bother you.

 c. If they are stupid enough to leave their diary out around somebody like you, they deserve to have it read.

 d. It will make you feel good to see how much they have always envied you.

 e. If you know your best friend's most em-barrassing secrets, it will be easier for you to get them to loan you money . . . again.

 f. Because you know that if you asked to read it, they would say no, so they are not really your best friend anyway.

7. When you're at a party and people richer, more attractive, and/or more popular than yourself snub you, you:

 a. Take their low opinion of you as a sign they are worth getting to know.

 b. Recognize that their low opinion of you demonstrates their excellent taste

and confirms your doubts about yourself.

c.   Try to seduce them so you can have the
satisfaction of criticizing their lack of
sexual prowess.

d.   Hope they get fat and develop a disfig-
uring skin disease so you can give them
cruel nicknames.

e.   Excuse yourself from the party and pee
on the door handle of their car.

f.   Tell everyone how much you like them
and that the rumors about their genital
warts are not true.

8.   When you look in the mirror, you see;
a.   Someone who deserves more.

b.   Someone who needs help.

c.   Someone who would be a better person
if there was money in it.

d.   Someone you would rather not have sex
with.

e.   Someone you wish you could have sex with.

f.   The most honest and loving person you
know.

9. When people compliment you, you:
    a. Wonder what they want from you.

    b. Know they are lying and/or being sarcastic.

    c. Think they are a bad judge of character and wonder how you can take advantage of their stupidity.

    d. Tell them they have great taste.

    e. Worry that you will now have to pay back the money you borrowed from them.

    f. Return the compliment in hopes you can get something from them.

10. When you look at this picture, you see:

    a. People you haven't met who can help you.

    b. People having fun at a party you're not invited to.

    c. You on your yacht in Saint Tropez surrounded by celebrity friends, with a hundred million dollars in your bank account.

    d.   A part of your body you should consider shaving.

    e.   All the lies you've told that make you seem more interesting.

    f.   All the people who wish they were you.

To score the test and find out what kind of social climber you are, add up the number of a, b, c, d, e, and f answers you have given.

If you have five or more "a" answers, you fall under the personality type we call a **Tactician**. You are, above all else, patient. Like a deer tick, you may wait a full year before attaching yourself to a warm-blooded creature who can carry you to the top. You are willing to become bosom buddies with six thoroughly unpleasant people in order to gain an introduction to the one person you really want to meet. As a child, you were good at making the most popular boy or girl in your class emotionally dependent on you. You know how to do just enough to seem like a better person than you are. You help others and generously volunteer small lies and alibis for recent acquaintances so when the time comes they will have to tell big lies for you.

Five or more "b" answers, you're what we call a **Velcro-Climber**. You have a God-given knack for attaching yourself to those who can advance you whether they like you or not. Your popularity has always stemmed from the fact that since you refuse to take a hint to get lost, you are impossible to ditch. By relentlessly inflicting your presence on others more popular, talented, and powerful than yourself, you wear down their defenses so that by the end of the evening, it is less exhausting for the somebodies of this world to let you hang with them than to keep running from you. Velcro-Climbers are often emotionally or physically impaired and are therefore skilled at making others feel guilty that they have more. Often, you enjoy playing the role of designated driver, and you are a skilled mixologist, which enables you to get people so drunk they have to let you drive them home.

Five or more "c" answers, you're what we call a **Go-Getter**. Being pushy comes naturally to you, you have always been aggressive toward people, especially those smaller and weaker than yourself. You want what others have, even if you don't want what they have. Usually, but not always, Go-Getters find themselves identifying with the shark on childhood trips to the aquarium. You are good at taking credit for other people's ideas and have always felt that those who lack the moral fortitude to lie and cheat deserve to be taken advantage of by people like yourself. Though the climbing techniques that come naturally to you are not subtle or pretty to watch, they are particularly effective for those trying to get ahead in New York City, Los Angeles, Third World dictatorships, or dystopian novels.

Five or more "d" answers, you're what we call the **Taste Meister**. You have always had the wisdom to value superficial things, people, and ideas. You understand the most pressing problems facing the world are not human rights, malnutrition, or the environmental crisis, but the ever-growing number of people with bad taste who are not using birth control. You believe that people who look intelligent and happy in photographs actually are, which is why you like to have your picture taken. You have been adept since childhood at covering up your lack of sophistication and creativity by convincing others you know more about being superficial than they do. You have always known how to make others feel dumb and boring for not buying or liking the same things that you do. Because Taste Meisters need money and/or power to inflict their bad taste on innocent bystanders, they often obtain rich and powerful girlfriends/ boyfriends/spouses and/or choose professions that enable them to spend extremely large sums of other people's money on objects that go out of fashion shortly after it's too late to return them.

Five or more "e" answers, you're what we call a **Mysterious Stranger**. People who have known you for years don't really know you, and you continually surprise yourself by your instinctive ability to exaggerate your accomplishments. Mysterious Strangers often, but not always, have an unusually honest face. This, coupled with a raconteur's gift for telling interesting stories about your life that never happened allows you to make new friends quickly. You have never let the truth get in the way of a good story, particularly if it makes you look good. Well-dressed unemployed foreigners and stylish individuals with fake accents and good table manners often fall into this "unknown" category.

Five or more "f" answers, you're what we call the **Good Old-Fashioned Phony**. People have always liked you because you tell them what they want to hear. You never say a bad word about anyone or anything. But beneath your sunny disposition, you have the good sense to always suspect the worst of others. Good Old-Fashioned Phonies often have freckles and unusually large eyes, features that make people inclined to make the mistake of trusting them. You are often perceived as naïve, idealistic, and good-hearted. Only you know you would have drowned kittens to get ahead. People don't realize how smart you are until you have stolen their friends and have outclimbed them.

Those whose answers indicate several kinds of personality traits should take comfort in the fact that they have the makings of a well-rounded Mountaineer. Those whose answers to nine or more questions fall into any single category should know you are truly special and, as such, should consider adjusting your medication and retaking this test.

4

DO I HAVE TO DITCH MY OLD FRIENDS TO MEET GLAMOROUS AND EXCITING NEW PEOPLE?

"Ditch" is an ugly word. We prefer to think of it as pruning the deadwood from the forest of your life so the new person you're about to become can grow tall. Or, as the Zen members of the social climbing community call it, practicing the art of "friend shui."

We understand that saying good-bye to lifelong friends and family members who will be a social liability can be hard. But honestly, do you really want your older brother hanging around telling Anna Wintour how you got the nickname Stinky?

Do you want that childhood friend who, after that first glass of Pinot Grigio, never fails to tell the story about the summer you gave crabs to all the lifeguards at Jones Beach tagging along with you to the polo matches in Bridgehampton?

EMPOWERING THOUGHT #7

Are your friends really your friends? Have you ever considered the possibility that your siblings and or childhood pals say embarrassing things about you because they have always resented you for being smarter, more talented, and more attractive than they are?

Couple that possibility with the fact that if you let them ride on your coattails and brought them along to all the fabulous places you'll be going, wouldn't they, in their heart of hearts, know that they, unlike you, don't belong? Isn't it even more obvious that they'd resent you for wanting to belong? Trust us, it is kinder and safer to delete them from your contacts before you even begin your climb.

The most difficult steps a fledgling Mountaineer has to take are the ones that come before he or she ever steps out the door and goes to the first party. Just as we asked you to take off your clothes and stand naked in front of the mirror to appraise your own physical assets, now it's time to cast a cold and unsentimental look at the people in your life.

Make a list of everyone you know. Relatives, friends, acquaintances, etc. Those who have more social entrée, access, or helpful friends than you do, mark as Keepers. Everyone else in your life is now a non-Keeper.

The odds are you will be shocked by how few Keepers you

have. Don't be discouraged. Try to remember the name of the girl who sat next to you in kindergarten who ate paste but whose family had a private plane. The hairless boy at sleepaway camp whom everybody made fun of for wetting his bed but went to Exeter. Yes, you made fun of him, too—but that doesn't mean you can't be friends now that you need him. He probably needs you, too.

Google search that great-aunt who called your grandfather white trash and has not spoken to your family since she married that Park Avenue surgeon or a Beverly Hills attorney. The chances are she'll enjoy hearing from you, especially if you volunteer that you now think your grandfather's white trash, too, and have followed her example and cut off contact with your family.

The world is a smaller place than you think. Be cheered by the fact that, at most, six degrees of separation lie between you and the kind of somebody who could change your life. Just to play it safe (without making it obvious), before ditching your old friends, casually inquire if they or any of their relations know anyone rich and/or famous. If so, make a point of getting them to introduce you to their somebodies before burning them with the rest of your personal deadwood.

Obviously, the deadwood in your life includes any individuals you are currently romantically involved with.

> You know better than anyone that if your boyfriend/girlfriend had anything going for them you wouldn't be turning to *The Social Climber's Bible* for comfort.

Once you have culled the non-Keepers from your social life, if the old crowd asks why you don't return their phone calls or hang out with them anymore at Hooters or the Olive Garden (or any other establishments you should never be caught dead in again, unless you are a climber who hopes to hang with the stars of *Duck Dynasty*), do not tell them the truth. Tell them you've given up drinking or are going to night school. If they persist, especially if the non-Keepers include family members, we strongly suggest moving to a different city and/or state.

Curiously enough, not knowing anybody in a new city can work to your advantage. The kind of creative embellishment of your backstory discussed in the previous chapter will be infinitely easier if you don't have to worry about people you grew up with constantly saying, "That's not true."

Everyone who moves to "the Big City," especially if they're in their twenties or early thirties, reinvents themselves. They try on different lifestyles and attitudes, expose themselves to types of people they never would have met had they stayed at home. The only difference between the civilian who comes to Gotham and makes new friends and the social climber is that the social climber makes new friends with a sense of purpose and a game plan.

EMPOWERING THOUGHT #8

Budding Mountaineers, new to the ways of the Big City, can still have dreams about how they want their life to turn out but never illusions about the friends and connections they'll need to obtain to make those dreams come true.

Know this: You aren't going to get to the top by befriending floundering fictional characters like those depicted in HBO's hit series *Girls*. The kinds of friends you need to make things happen for you in real life are the supremely well-connected actresses who portray those girls.

The multitalented star Lena Dunham, who's also the creator, writer, director, and producer of *Girls*, is the child of two highly accomplished artists who knew everyone who was anyone in the culture ghetto of New York, plus: designer Zac Posen was her babysitter, and she graduated from the elite private school Saint Ann's. Equally well-connected Zosia Mamet, aka Shoshanna Shapiro, happens to be the daughter of Pulitzer Prize–winning playwright, screenwriter, and director David Mamet. Marnie Michaels, played by Allison Williams, graduated from Yale and is lucky enough to be the daughter of NBC's star anchorman Brian Williams. And last but not least, Jemima Kirke, who plays Jessa Johansson and also attended Saint Ann's, has a double whammy going for her: She's the child of a rock star (Bad Company's Simon Kirke) and the granddaughter of a London billionaire, "Black Jack" Dellal.

If you, like 99.9 percent of the world, do not have the good fortune to have as famous, talented, well-connected, and rich parents as the girls on *Girls* do, and weren't lucky, privileged, or smart enough to attend private schools or matriculate at Ivy League universities, don't waste time envying or resenting those with more: Get to know them!

If you are starting out from social ground zero and have just moved to a new city and literally know no one and do not have a job that will bring you in touch with anyone or anything remotely fabulous, the first and most important thing for you to do is get off Facebook and any and all social websites, dating services, chat rooms, etc. that you are in any way connected to.

Why?

An old posting, a snapshot, for example, of you flashing your ta-tas back on spring break of '10, admitting "liking" Justin Bieber, or any one of the embarrassing things and people you used to "like" before you decided to become a social climber could be as much a liability as those indiscreet friends and family you have already cut out of your new life.

> Purge any and all embarrassing details and indiscretions from cyberspace, to make sure your past does not sabotage your future.

For now, leave your virtual life a blank canvas. When you have acquired enough exciting friends and photos of yourself doing cool and extraordinary things to make it appear to those more connected than yourself that you are more popular and successful than you are, we will show you how to fill up the blank canvas of your life with such verve and panache you won't recognize yourself.

But between then and now, we have a lot of work to do.

Here are some practical and affordable first steps that will put upwardly mobile strangers new to a city in a position where they can become best buddies with someone who can help them step into the winner's circle.

1. Get a list of all the Alcoholics Anonymous, Al-Anon, and Narcotics Anonymous meetings offered in your city and start attending those that are held in the basements of churches, community centers, or public spaces in the hippest, most exclusive and expensive neighborhoods. Every one of America's first families has at least one heir or heiress with a substance abuse problem. Just look at the Kennedys. Take note of those in recovery who are accessorized with twenty-thousand-dollar Hermès Kelly bags and have not succumbed to hocking their Rolex watches and five-carat Tiffany diamond studs to buy crack or go on a bender. Listen carefully when those struggling with their addictions begin to share—those who have fallen off the wagon at the Times Square Blarney Stone are not Keepers. Those who make reference to having recently backslid at exclusive golf and country clubs, hot restaurants, or exotic resorts are Keepers. Being in recovery, they could use and will be genuinely grateful for a responsible new friend like yourself.

    Note: If you are already in the program, better still! Becoming the sponsor of a derelict with a large trust fund or a Master of the Universe with an OxyContin problem can change the whole trajectory of your climb. If your recovering Big Fish accuses you of being pushy when you insist on accompanying him or her to a social function they don't want to bring you to, you can honestly say that you are insisting on riding on their coattails simply to safeguard their sobriety.

2. Check the pages of the newspaper online every day for memorial services open to the public to celebrate the lives of recently deceased statesmen, captains of industry, celebrities, and society figures who never would have deigned to talk to you while they were alive. You'll be surprised: The bigger the dead fish, the more likely the memorial will be open to the public. Dead rich and famous people have famous friends who are still alive and can help you.

Remember to arrive early enough to get a seat just behind the section in the cathedral, synagogue, or mosque that is reserved for family. Dress properly. Weep discreetly and you'll have a better than fifty-fifty chance, as the anthropologists put it, of "making first contact" with a member of the tribe you want to join, especially if you recognize someone from all those AA meetings you've been attending.

Being grief-stricken, those who actually knew the deceased will be unlikely to press you for specifics as to when and where you met their late, great friend. As always, do your homework and read the obits carefully. If the deceased had an affection for Scottish terriers, say you went to the Westminster dog show together. If the departed had a ski house in the Alps and died in an avalanche, say you met them in the deep powder of Val D'Isère. Those who live in New York City and are not squeamish should make a habit of popping into the Frank E. Campbell Funeral Chapel on Madison Avenue to see who has checked out and checked in. Open-casket viewings of a dead Big Fish always attract a good crowd.

3. Upscale art gallery openings are also a perfect place to make the acquaintance of your first Big Fish.

> Those willing to drop 400K for a work on paper with as little concern as you have springing for extra cheese on a sandwich are the kind of people you want to get to know.

Plus, at art gallery openings, they hand out free glasses of white wine. A word to the wise: Before imbibing, make sure none of your friends from AA are there. If you see someone you recognize from the memorial service or from your trip to the funeral home, make a point of greeting them with a hug and a heart-felt, "I can't believe our friend's not with us any-more." Ask for a price list from one of the attractive young men or women who work in the gallery. If this is New York City, they will be rude to you. Mention your financial advisor wants to start diversifying your portfolio into the contemporary art market and they will probably still be rude to you, but it will plant a seed of uncertainty regarding your place in the food chain, which you will be able to build upon when you get to your next cultural freebie.

4. The art auctions at Sotheby's, Christie's, Parke-Bernet, etc., are also open to the public. During the big sales, the rich, the powerful, and the famous descend on them to do just what you're doing—social climbing—but we will have more to say on Kunst climbing later. For now, look around for people who ignored you at the memorial services and the art gallery openings you've been attending. Strange but true: You will no longer be a deadbeat if you raise your paddle and bid against Peter Brant, the polo-playing billionaire art collector/industrialist husband of aging supermodel Stephanie Seymour for a $120 million dead shark floating in formalde-hyde signed by Damien Hirst. Now the gallery assistants who didn't believe you had a financial advisor will not only

make a point of introducing you to the artist they're showing at the next opening, they'll also invite you to the swank
and exclusive dinner that will invariably be held afterward.
Word of caution: Stay in the bidding long enough to be no-
ticed, but drop out in time to avoid being arrested for making the winning bid on a $120 million dead fish when you
only have sixteen dollars in your bank account.

5.   There isn't a Church of Upward Mobility . . . yet.

> Social climbing in the right house of worship will not only
> bring you closer to heaven, it can make your prayers come
> true.

Every major city in the world has one special church,
cathedral, temple, or mosque where the elite absolve themselves of the sins they committed to get where they are. Find
the powerhouse of faith in your city and start praying—you
never know who will be on their knees next to you at holiday
time. Casually mention that due to a foul-up with airlines,
you can't fly home for Christmas, Yom Kippur, or Ram-
adan, and you just might find yourself breaking bread with
a Big Fish.

For those who live in California, especially
readers with aspirations in the entertainment
industry, the Church of Scientology is of course
a viable alternative. But we must caution those

who are considering the L. Ron Hubbard route in their climb—with Scientology there is always the risk that before you can start climbing, you'll have to spend a year or two putting starch in John Travolta's briefs.

6. Do your homework. Memorize the names and faces pictured on the party pages of *Vanity Fair*, *Vogue*, *New York Magazine*, or that glossy city mag that's published in whatever metropolis you currently reside in. Keep track of who and what social functions appear in the Style section of the *New York Times* and *W* magazine. Check out Bill Cunningham's "Evening Hours" pics, *New York Social Diary*, and society shutterbug Patrick McMullan's website. Monitor those mentioned in gossip columns like "Page Six" and in the society rags like *Avenue*, *Hamptons Magazine*, *South Beach Magazine*, and so on. By the time you finish reading this book, many of the names and faces that appear in them will already be déclassé, but they will still be able to introduce you to people who aren't.

> Remember, there is nothing wrong with claiming to be friends with boldface celebs you haven't met, but only amateurs drop their first names.

With hard work, a little luck, and a few liberties with reality at the above-mentioned events, you might have the good fortune to have already stumbled upon what every social climber needs—a new best friend who will serve as your champion, Sherpa, and guide.

As a social climber who's just starting off, you will have many rivers to cross, some so wide and treacherous, so filled with obstacles, they might take years to traverse—unless you find someone willing to carry you on their back. People who provide this service fall into two categories, which we like to refer to as Turtles and Swans.

Turtles are individuals who have social resources they are too shy, awkward, and insecure to take advantage of or exploit on their own, i.e., Turtles are unlike you. Sometimes, but not always, they are inhibited by a physical handicap other than their shell— a lisp, a stutter, a limp, a case of acne that makes them resemble a parboiled parrot. But a good Turtle always has parents and/or grandparents who possess at least two of the following: old money, new money, artistic accomplishment, international renown, political prominence (senator, governor, cabinet minister), or an inherited title.

Often, but not always, Turtles are accomplished in their own right, but their shells are so thick and isolating they are unable to or unaware of how to take advantage of their position in the world. Doors have been open to them their whole lives. But being Turtlelike, they're too fearful to come out of their shells and cross over to assume their rightful place on the other side of the velvet rope—that is, until you climb on their back and steer them in the right direction.

The relationship between you and your Turtle is not exploitative. Your Turtle is not a beast of burden. Your Turtle takes you to the party, but you show him how to have a good time and introduce him to all the new and exciting people you wouldn't have met without him. A smart social climber is always nice to the Turtle; unlike fleas or other parasites, you do not feed off your Turtle, you devour the good life together.

As you become a more accomplished climber, in all likelihood you will acquire more than one Turtle. When that happens, you must always remember to make each Turtle feel special. Though the relationship can become so intimate that your reflection will virtually be painted on your Turtle's shell, you should never, never, never have sex with your Turtle. You won't be tempted, but your Turtle will, even if you are average-looking.

When your friendship with your Turtles has given them the newfound self-confidence to bring up the subject of sex (and they will), soften your rejection by telling them you love them like a brother or sister and introduce them to people who like to have sex with Turtles but have no social ambitions of their own. If you do not know anyone who will fit this bill, you can meet them by attending a Sex Addicts Anonymous meeting.

Whereas Turtles are slow, unattractive, and reliable rides, Swans, both the male and the female of this subspecies of social transport, are as unpredictable as they are unnaturally beautiful. Swans are usually but not always models, actors, or actresses. Being Swans, i.e., gorgeous, they are invited everywhere—in part because rich and powerful people who throw parties want to have sex with them, but more often simply because Big Fish want to make their friends *think* they have had sex with them. Swans are sometimes but not always less intelligent and less socially connected than Turtles. But there are exceptions, i.e., "It" girls, who are female Swans with jobs in the fashion industry that don't pay enough for them to afford to get fatter than a size four.

Swans will be happy to bring someone as average as yourself to a social function, either a) because they are so beautiful they are insecure that they have nothing else to offer, or b) because if they appear to have a date, it'll be easier for them to say no to their host's or hostess's sexual advances without offending them.

But know this about Swans: Yes, it's fun to ride on such gorgeous backs, but you are not their "date." They have brought you to the party because if they meet someone who can advance their careers or make them forget the heartbreak of being so beautiful, they can fly off without having to say good-bye and/or inform you that you are being dumped for the night.

Though Swans are not listed in the DSM, many psychiatrists categorize them as borderline personality types. Whether that is fact or vengeful thinking on the part of the members of the medical profession who do not get to ride Swans is open to debate. But implicit in the symbiotic relationship between Swans and social climbers is the unspoken understanding that, though the Swans may hold your hand, grind themselves provocatively against your nether regions on the dance floor, call you Darling, and say they love you, they know you're a social climber, not a real date.

> You, like everyone else, will want to have sex with your Swan. Do not sleep with your Swan.

Due to the fact that they are as lacking in self-esteem as the Turtles, when they are depressed or bored, they might even suggest an unnatural coupling. Resist. The surest way to lose your Swan is to sleep with him or her. Why? Because when you add sex to the equation, Swans will know that you, just like everybody else, want to use them.

5 | TEST YOUR SOCIAL CLIMBING IQ

Even if you scored well enough on our psychological test to indicate that you have a personality ideally suited for Mountaineering, and are fortunate enough to already have met a Swan or a Turtle who is ready, willing, and able to take you somewhere you want to go, before you step out the door we have one final homework assignment for you to complete. The following test will help you determine what rung of the ladder you're ready to reach for.

1. What's the first thing you do when you get to a cocktail party where you don't know anyone?

   a) Ask your host to introduce you to someone who might want to sleep with you.

   b) Pretend you see a friend across the room and wave to someone you don't know.

    c)   Head to the bar and get bombed to make yourself feel less like a loser.

    d)   Introduce yourself to someone who is also being ignored.

2.   When is it the "right time" to tell a Big Fish you find them sexually attractive?

    a)   When you can't pay your rent.

    b)   After the Big Fish has given you a Ferrari.

    c)   Never.

    d)   As soon as the Big Fish tells you they are getting divorced.

3)   What is the best way for a nobody to get into the hottest nightclub on the planet?

    a)   Borrow a couture outfit and offer the doorman/woman a hundred dollars.

    b)   Shave your head and say the Make-A-Wish Foundation put you on the guest list.

    c)   Claim you are bringing medication to a celebrity you saw enter previously.

    d)   Lurk in the gutter and look for under-age wealthy Whale spawn and tell the doorman/woman you are their chaperone.

4) Which of the following will *not* help you make friends with celebrities?

> a) A baby cheetah bite.
>
> b) Make him/her paranoid by telling them that their other friends want them to get fat.
>
> c) Knowledge of bowling.
>
> d) Inviting them to your home.

5) Which of the following will help the social climbing golfer get into a WASP country club?

> a) Being a scratch golfer and having $100 million.
>
> b) Having a beautiful wife.
>
> c) Looking as if he/she is constipated.
>
> d) Using big words in an interview with the membership committee.

6) Which of the following do you need to know when flying on a private jet?

> a) If you are caught bringing drugs on board the Whale's plane, they will be confiscated.
>
> b) Altitudes in excess of thirty thousand feet produce flatulence in miniature dogs.

     c)   If you are the last on board and the flight is full, you will be sitting on a well-upholstered toilet.

     d)   All of the above.

7) What should the social climber *never* do at a charity dinner?

     a)   Change the *placemente* when no one is looking.

     b)   Pay for his or her own ticket.

     c)   Give the false impression that he or she is on the benefit committee.

     d)   Eat other people's lamb chops.

8) Skilled networkers should:

     a)   Replace their mentors as often as they update their software.

     b)   Always question the intelligence of a Big Fish who is eager to help them.

     c)   Not complain if asked to take their bosses' urine samples to the lab.

     d)   All of the above.

9) When the yachting set uses the word "burgee," they are referring to:

     a)   A guest who is sleeping with the yacht owner while on board.

b) A guest who likes to sleep with crew members.

c) A small flag that indicates which yacht club the owner is a member of.

d) The enclosed structure at the stern of the ship above the main deck.

10) What is the best way to ingratiate yourself with a wealthy family?

a) Make a good impression on their dogs.

b) Agree with them when they complain about their staff.

c) Volunteer to provide an alibi if one of them gets arrested.

d) Tell them you want to be adopted.

11) Friendship with which of the following will give a social climber the most status?

a) The CEO of a Fortune 500 company.

b) A supermodel with a reputation for promiscuity.

c) The maître d' at the hottest restaurant in town.

d) The head of admissions at an Ivy League college.

12) When a social climber is a guest for the weekend, which of the following is socially unforgivable?

    a)   Clogging the powder room toilet and blaming it on the host's/hostess's child.

    b)   Double-faulting when playing doubles in tennis.

    c)   Forgetting to tip the maid.

    d)   Soiling the sheets with bodily fluids other than your own.

Answer Key: 1) b, 2) c, 3) d, 4) d, 5) c, 6) d, 7) b, 8) d, 9) c, 10) a, 11) d, 12) b

If you answered 0–3 questions correctly, face up to the fact that you need help and visit our website to arrange an online tutoring session.

If you answered 4–7 questions correctly, with a little work, you have the makings of a great climber.

If you answered 8–10 questions correctly, you are a natural Mountaineer, or live in New York City.

If you answered 11 or more questions correctly, you cheated. And we say good for you, because initiative is part of what makes a good social climber.

6 |

HOW TO GET MORE OUT OF A COCKTAIL PARTY THAN A HANGOVER

A shrewd social climber looks at a roomful of total strangers with drinks in their hands the way a prospector eyes a mother lode untouched by other gold diggers. Think of those strangers who more than likely will take no notice of your arrival not as people but as opportunities waiting to be mined—every one of them an unwitting accomplice in changing your life.

If you're nervous, draw strength from the fact that as they size you up and judge you, you are doing the same to them.

EMPOWERING THOUGHT #9

In social climbing, as in life, the healthiest way to cope with an awkward feeling is to "flip it"—confidence comes to those who have mastered the art of projecting their own insecurities onto others.

Those unsuspecting strangers who are getting tipsy, oblivious to the knowledge that you are mastering the lessons of *The Social Climber's Bible*—they are the ones who should be nervous, not you.

Cocktail parties were invented for social climbing.

Cocktail parties are the most cost-effective way for a host to entertain the largest possible number of people in a three- to four-hour time period. Some guests will be old friends of your host. Most will be what we call "obligations," those your host has included as payback for being allowed to climb at their parties. Others, like yourself, fall into the acquaintance category.

For you, the cocktail party is an audition. Your host is trying you out, in WASP-speak, "sizing up the cut of your jib," seeing if you bring enough to the table in terms of charm, flattery, ability to make scintillating conversation, witty repartee, and so forth for your host to invest more time in you, that is, invite you to the five-course seated dinner he's throwing next month to impress a big client, or make the new fiancée think his friend group is more fascinating than it really is.

Regardless of whether the guests you now have to face, the strangers who have crowded into a room to drink alcohol and exchange gossip without the benefit of adequate seating, are standing on wall-to-wall shag or spilling drinks and dropping finger food on eighteenth-century Aubusson carpets, no matter if this cocktail party (what the English refer to as a "drinks party") takes place in a suburban backyard, the garden of a country estate, the terrace of an NYC penthouse, or around an infinity pool in LA, the same basic rules apply when it comes to the social climber's getting the most out of the cocktail party experience.

For the virgin as well as the veteran social climber, it's always a good idea to remind yourself before leaving home that you aren't simply getting ready to go to a cocktail party, you're preparing yourself to step onto the battlefield.

The most successful strategy at a drinks party combines elements of both trench warfare and the hit-and-run techniques of guerrilla fighting. Due to time and space limitations, your maneuvers at most cocktail skirmishes will be confined to a few rooms: living room, den or library, bar area (usually the dining room), and one or two bathrooms, which should be used only for strategic retreat, unless of course you are attending a cocktail party where drugs are being consumed.

The close quarters of a cocktail party can work to your advantage in stalking the Big Fish; it will enable you to rub shoulders without spooking them.

Be smart, be aggressive, and never give up until the bar closes.

Remember, all it takes is one conquest to change the course of the war you're waging—to turn an evening of what seems like certain defeat into total victory.

If any or all of the above makes you more nervous, before leaving home have what one well-known social climber described to us as the "Lake Placid moment," a chemical refuge of serenity and focus induced by a glass of Sancerre with a Xanax floater. In general, we strongly advise against "pregaming," or starting the party too early; remember, you have a busy night ahead of you.

Cocktail Party Prep List

1. Before leaving home, google your host/hostess so you will know what they will brag about ahead of time.
2. Give yourself a once-over (especially important if you've had more than one Lake Placid moment while getting dressed).
3. Check to make sure there is no food in your teeth and that your fly is zipped, unless you are going to the kind of event where this is a good conversation starter.
4. If you intend to take off your underwear in the course of the evening, make sure that the pair that you are wearing does not contain holes and is not stained.
5. Never arrive at the cocktail party less than thirty minutes late (unless you are triply booked).
6. Leave your credit cards at home, so if invited to an impromptu dinner afterward with people you just met you will have a good reason not to pay your share of the bill.
7. Bring your cellphone so you can record the names of Big Fish you meet before you get too drunk to remember them.

When you arrive, never ring the bell or knock; it makes it seem as if you are unsure if you're wanted. Take a deep breath before opening the door and repeat your mantra, "I CARE ENOUGH ABOUT ME NOT TO BELIEVE ANYTHING

THEY SAY ABOUT ME IS TRUE IF I DON'T WANT IT TO BE. I WILL NOT BE JUDGED."

Once inside, if in fact you do not know anyone other than your host, do not let your body language reveal you're an outsider. Stand on tiptoes and look around as if you were trying to spot an old friend. Wave enthusiastically to a total stranger on the other side of the room to make it seem as if you know someone.

A variation of this same basic technique can also be used whenever you are stuck in a conversation with someone who cannot help you and you don't know how to escape. Take a page from a well-known former nineties "It"-girl-turned-luxury-goods-garmento (who, to avoid litigation, we'll simply refer to as Meme) who never goes to a party without her imaginary friend Hercules to come to her rescue. How can an imaginary friend help you? When Meme wants to get out of small talk that has no self-promotion potential, i.e., wants to be rude without seeming to be rude, she merely says, "Oh, there's my friend Hercules. He doesn't know anyone; you don't mind if I look after him, do you?"

EMPOWERING THOUGHT #10

If you are worried that you are not as attractive as other guests, pause to focus on the one part of your body that is unique—a birthmark shaped like the Dominican Republic or a third nipple—as proof that you are special and beautiful.

Before proceeding any farther into the room, check to see if anyone you recognize from those AA meetings, memorial services, art gallery openings, and auctions where you placed bogus bids is present in the room.

If your host is still the only person you know, wait until he or she is talking to at least two interesting-looking people (expensively accessorized or so badly dressed they obviously have to be somebodies for your host not to have been offended by their attire) before interrupting to say hello. Always begin by announcing how fabulous they look and how much you miss and love them.

> Never underestimate the value of kissing your hosts on all four of their cheeks.

And remember, when your host or hostess introduces you to these first two strangers (and when meeting anyone else for the first time), never, never say, "It's a pleasure to meet you." The graceful social climber always greets a stranger with: "So nice to see you again. . . ."

By giving the illusion that you have met before, you will be that much closer to actually having a genuine friendship. Getting into the strict habit of never acknowledging you haven't met everyone and anyone will be invaluable in future years when you have more friends than you can keep track of. Why? Because it will also prevent you from falling into the embarrassing trap of saying "So nice to meet you" and being told by the offended party, "I've met you a dozen times," or worse, "We slept together . . . twice."

You now know not one but three people. Unless one of these first two people your host has just introduced you to is a major Big Fish, after ten minutes of your best small talk, excuse yourself to go to the bar. Your time is precious; do the math. There are seventy-five other people in the room; the party starts at six, runs to nine. Having arrived thirty minutes late, then spending ten minutes chatting up your host and your two new best friends, you have less than two and a half hours left to make a favorable impression on the remaining seventy-two guests. A word to the wise—even if your day job includes waiting on tables and even if the request is made by a major, major Big Fish, do not waste your time getting anyone a drink unless they are a potential Turtle or Swan. Besides the fact it will put you in a subservient role in any future relationship, your time at this ball is more limited than Cinderella's.

> Never walk directly to the bar.

In fact, take the longest route possible. You are not going to get a drink, you're on a reconnaissance mission. If no one is talking to you, look busy. Check the messages on your cellphone, or study the negative space of a painting on the wall. While doing this, be on the lookout for groups clustered around single individuals who are holding court—take note of guests hanging on every word of somebody who isn't saying anything very interesting, laughing at jokes that aren't funny, particularly if the object of their attention is not physically attractive. The conclusion you should draw is obvious—whoever's receiving this unwarranted fawning is a somebody, i.e., somebody you should want to get to know.

If you do not recognize this somebody from the homework you've done, loiter around the edge of the adoring throng long enough to catch the somebody's name. If all you hear is, "Oh, Johnny, you're such a scream!" and can't pick up any clues as to who this Johnny is and what makes him such a scream, look for an older person to help you, ideally somebody who is confined to a wheelchair and is also being ignored. Never miss an opportunity to seem more empathetic than you are. Introduce yourself to the oldie, make just enough small talk about their ailments to cheer them up, then work the conversation round to the identity of the mysterious Johnny. Of course, don't admit to the old person that you're so uncool that you don't know who this somebody is, simply say you cannot remember Johnny's surname.

An equally good and generally undervalued source of information is the child of your host or hostess. If the child knows Johnny's full name but neither of you know what makes him such a hot ticket, pass on the bar and get yourself and your iPhone directly to the powder room and google the name you've just been given.

Having found out who he is and what makes him a Big Fish, return to where Johnny is holding court and volunteer, "I thought your first [movie/play/novel/merger/ad campaign/class action suit/whatever] was beyond brilliant." Remember to include enough details so they will actually believe you have been following their career for years.

> **EMPOWERING THOUGHT #11**
> Highly accomplished people never get tired of hearing how great they are, no matter what they tell their shrinks.

Do not waste time eating hors d'oeuvres, unless that somebody you've just googled is cracking wise over the canapés. Do not be so dazzled and distracted by obvious somebodies that you miss out on befriending the seemingly less impressive guests who are, in fact, hidden nuggets of gold. Remember: You are first and foremost a prospector. Experienced social climbers make every party their party by deliberately introducing themselves to every person at the party, just in case there's what we call a "Sleeper" in the room.

People who look like they work at the Foot Locker often do in fact work as a shoe salesperson. But sometimes they also look that way because they own a global chain of shoe stores, and they just might find you such good company and so seemingly genuine for taking the time to befriend a nebbish such as themselves, that they just might invite you to the Gangnam-style grand opening of their new flagship store in Seoul, South Korea.

THE THREE QUESTIONS YOU NEVER WANT TO ASK AT A COCKTAIL PARTY

1. Who are you?
2. Where do you live?
3. What do you do?

Why? Because asking any of the above will indelibly mark you as an obvious social climber. Of course you need to know the answers to these questions before you waste time on someone who can't help you, but there are much more polite ways to be rude. We have already told you how to avoid asking people directly who they are by consulting geriatrics, children, and Google. A more gracious way of finding out whether a fellow guest lives, say, in a Fifth Avenue penthouse versus a rent-controlled studio in Staten Island is to ask, "Don't you live in TriBeCa?" Nine times out of ten, regardless of whether they are residents of TriBeCa, the question will prompt them to tell you exactly where they do live.

As to question #3, "What do you do?," which, after all, really translates into "How much do you make?," is more tactfully handled by making a supposition: "Aren't you in finance?" If you are right, they will proceed to tell you what firm they work for and just how big a big shot they are, and if they are not in finance, they will either be flattered or insulted by your false assumption and proceed to tell you exactly what they do do and why you should be impressed.

There is no need to waste time inquiring whether someone at the cocktail party attended Harvard, Yale, or Princeton, for the simple reason that if they had, they will find an excuse to casually drop that particular of their resume at least twice before you tell them to stop eating all of the cashews out of the mixed nut bowl.

Determining whether someone is a total waste of time takes time. In all of the interactions mentioned above, maintain eye contact; do not gaze over the shoulder of the person you are talking to to look for an even bigger fish. Yes, you must keep your eyes peeled for a better opportunity, but you don't want to put off possible Sleepers by making them wonder if you're looking over their shoulders because you are bored or possibly worried federal marshals are about to burst into the room and arrest you.

At a certain point during every urbane cocktail party, the observant climber will notice a group of middle-aged, well-dressed women standing around glancing at their watches impatiently and looking bored while their Big Fish husbands hold forth and tell stale stories their wives can no longer bear to hear, much less laugh at.

The ignored wives of somebodies are an all too often overlooked opportunity for social advancement. Caution: If you are a straight man paying undue attention to the ignored wife, you will alienate the Big Fish husband. Even if they haven't slept in the same bed for years, even if the Big Fish has arranged for his mistress to attend this cocktail party, the Big Fish, being an alpha male, will still be territorial when it comes to straight strangers flattering their missus. But a Big Fish husband is more than happy to see a young woman or gay man chatting up his wife, if for no other reason than it means he won't have to hear her complain about being ignored all night when they get home.

If you are a gay man or a heterosexual woman, take advantage of any and all opportunities to become new best friends with the long-suffering wife of a powerful man. Invite the wife to lunch, bring her to your gym, take her on a shopping spree in a part of town where she won't feel entirely safe. Offer to babysit her children for free. Soon, the ignored wife will be inviting you to their house. Because she's lonely, she'll make you an honorary member of the family. Xmas presents, free trips, and job opportunities from hubby will follow. The kiddies will start to call you Auntie or Uncle.

Single women or gay men, if so inclined, are then in the perfect position to put a dying marriage out of its misery by running off with the husband and becoming the next spouse of Mr. Big Fish. This is what we call the Bait and Switch technique.

Regardless of whether that technique is for you, by the end of your first cocktail party (if you follow our instructions), you will have made so many new and useful friends that you will very likely be invited to tag along to an impromptu dinner or after-party.

This spur-of-the-moment get-together will undoubtedly be an occasion where more cocktails will be consumed. Because you might very well end up at a nightclub where there will be still more cocktails, and after getting down with your bad self on the dance floor, you just might be tempted to take a nightcap shot of tequila along with a hit of X, which of course could possibly land you in bed with a person far more socially connected than yourself . . . we urge you to read the following chapter twice before going to your first cocktail party.

7

SEX AND THE SOCIAL CLIMBER

At some point in your climb you will be tempted to give your most precious gift, yourself, to a Big Fish for one of three reasons: a) an overwhelming physical attraction (unlikely); b) genuine romantic feelings (also unlikely); c) because you think sex will inspire Mr./Ms./Mrs. Big Fish to be nicer to you and therefore do more to help you move up in the world. Regardless of the nature of your desires, there are certain facts of life that have nothing to do with the birds and the bees that you should know.

Yes, for social climbers of any and all genders and regardless of sexual orientation, having sex with a portal to a brighter future—getting nasty with someone vastly more connected and influential than yourself—can take you to the top of the ladder literally overnight. But there are risks other than STDs for the Mountaineer who chooses that method of climbing.

EMPOWERING THOUGHT #12

Where sexual desires are concerned, especially when love is involved, you are not in control; your desires control you. Since a good social climber is always in control, sex and worse, love, can lead to potentially fatal missteps.

For those considering making use of sex in their climb, always remember this: The wise climber never makes the first sexual overture to a Big Fish. We say that not because we are prudish or old-fashioned, but simply because if they are a Big Fish, and you're a guppy, particularly if you are a very young and attractive guppy and they are old and scaly, if you hit on them first, they will be prone to suspect that you are interested in them for reasons other than their body.

EMPOWERING THOUGHT #13

A social climber should never seem like a gold digger, especially if he or she is one.

Be meek, coy, modest, claim to be a semivirgin, swear you've never taken a shower before with anyone in your life. Even if they don't believe it, they'll find it exciting to hear you say it.

What to do when the Big Fish hits on you? Every Mountaineer has to decide for themselves when it's right to say yes, no, and maybe. First and foremost, social climbers should never allow anyone to put them in a situation where they feel pressured or obligated to have sex. Even if the Big Fish has given you a job, a Ferrari, or a ten-carat diamond, you still have the right to say no. Though perhaps if you've been given all three, it might be wise to say, "Maybe someday I'll feel that way about you, but for right now, let's just keep on being friends."

Surprisingly, in general there are far more reasons to say no than yes to sex. If you are less than gorgeous/subhandsome, i.e., the average person, you know that sex *can* be a beautiful thing . . . but often, it is not. Because Big Fish of both sexes possess large egos to hide equally oversized insecurities, if you sleep with a Big Fish, and the sex is bad/awkward/weird or fails to end in liftoff for the Big Fish, who is most likely to be blamed for the disappointment? YOU!

Even if your Big Fish has the honesty to admit that he's always been a premature ejaculator, or confessed the closest thing she's ever had to an orgasm occurred in a previous life, chances are they will be so embarrassed by their confession they not only won't want to try having sex with you again, they won't want to see you again, i.e., you won't be invited to their next party.

Now if the sex is great for the Big Fish but leaves you feeling less than satisfied, or as if you've just been slimed by a giant slug, you will be in an even worse position. Why? Because now the Big Fish is going to want to have sex with you again, and again, and again. Instead of taking you to those fantastic parties that enabled you to meet the Big Fish's even Bigger Fish friends, your Big Fish is going to want to keep you all to him- or herself so he/she can have more sex. Say good-bye to all those glamorous dinners at chic restaurants where you could table hop. You will find yourself trapped in romantic rendezvous in out-of-the-way, dimly lit bistros, or worse, staying in and having takeout and yes, more sex. In short, don't set yourself up to be a sore loser . . . literally.

Surprising but true, that small minority of readers who are above average in physical appearance or drop-dead gorgeous/Adonis handsome often find themselves in an even more abusive and disadvantaged position. Beautiful women who refuse to have sex with an ardent male Big Fish, who have the self-respect and honesty to say a simple "No, thank you," are nine times out of ten subsequently told that they are cold, heartless bitches and/or lesbians. Which isn't so bad if you are a lesbian. Except if that is the case, the rejected Big Fish will then pester you to let him watch while you have sex with one of his girlfriends.

Similarly, when an extremely handsome man declines the sexual overtures of a female Big Fish, he of course is immediately labeled "gay." Which sometimes might be the case. But even if you are extremely handsome and gay and the Big Fish is gay and you say, "Thanks but no thanks" to having him for dinner, you, like the beautiful woman, will also be called a "bitch."

The safest and surest way to avoid landing in a sexual position that could either jeopardize or sidetrack social advancement is to put yourself from the get-go in a position where you won't ever have to say yes, no, or maybe. How do you do that? Simple. The first time the subtext of sex comes up, simply say, "I'd love to, but I just had this surgical procedure. . . ." Make it clear that it's nothing contagious or so serious as to force you to close shop forever. Just a small plumbing problem that will rule out any attempt at intercourse for the next six months. In the meantime, you'll be free to flirt, flatter, and kiss as many frogs as necessary to get where you want to go.

We strongly suggest that those readers who still think they have what it takes to climb the ladder via a series of sexual conquests go back to the mirror and remove their clothes. If after a second naked, hard look at yourself, you are still convinced you have the physical assets and moral elasticity to screw your way to the top, hats off to you and remember the following:

a) While many Big Fish of both sexes will be impressed if you have had an affair with the likes of Mick Jagger, Rihanna, Tom Cruise, Rachel Maddow, or Taylor Swift, and will be intrigued by your previous romantic attachment to someone richer and more powerful than themselves, boasting you had a quickie in the bathroom stall of a nightclub with such luminaries will be decidedly less impressive.

b) Never admit to anyone, much less yourself, that you had sex with someone to gain entrée, access, or a free ride on a G7.

c) Social climbers don't sleep around, they simply fall in love easily with men and/or women who by mere coincidence always seem to be very rich, very famous, and/or very generous.

An informative role model for our female readers who want to Mountaineer while remaining horizontal is Pamela Harriman, aka the Whale Huntress.

Marriage #1: At nineteen, Harriman is set up on a blind date with Winston Churchill's son, Randolph; she tells him he will recognize her because she is "chubby." Despite the fact that Randolph is known for getting drunk and asking all of his first dates to marry him, three days later they are officially engaged.

Moral: Great social climbers do not let average looks or the substance abuse problems of their mates get in the way of a good ride. Also, they do not stop dating up the food chain just because they are married. . . .

Affairs While Married to Randolph

Averell Harriman—Union Pacific heir.

Jock Whitney—Owner of the *New York Herald Tribune*.

Bill Paley—President of CBS.

Edward R. Murrow—World-renowned journalist.

Moral: A great social climber who is married does not stop trying to move up in the world. (Unfortunately, Pamela was unable to get any of the above boyfriends to leave their wives.)

Affairs After Divorcing Randolph

Gianni Agnelli—Heir to the Fiat automotive fortune.

Marquis Alfonso de Portago—Spanish millionaire, playboy, and race car driver.

Prince Aly Khan—Millionaire racehorse owner and future husband of Rita Hayworth.

Stavros Niarchos—Greek shipping tycoon.

Baron Élie de Rothschild—Heir to the French banking fortune.

Frank Sinatra—(This affair cannot be confirmed, but he was definitely in her "friend" group.)

Moral: A great social climber knows that once you sleep with one Whale, other Whales will want to sleep with you, too.

Marriage #2: Harriman marries Leland Heyward, legendary Broadway producer of such hits as *South Pacific.* Unfortunately, when Heyward dies, Pamela is horrified to discover that after she had actually been faithful to him, he left half of his meager fortune to his children by his previous marriage.

Moral: Even great social climbers experience setbacks.

Marriage #3: Pamela discovers the third time is truly lucky. Averell Harriman, the Whale who got away, marries her six months after his wife dies. His fortune enables her to become the number one fund-raiser for the Democratic Party. Young Whale president Bill Clinton thanks her for her largess by making her ambassador to France. Befitting one of the greatest Mountaineers ever, she dies swimming laps in the pool of the Ritz Hotel in Paris. As was once said of Harriman, "She was a world expert on rich men's bedroom ceilings."

Moral: If you don't succeed at first, try, try, and try again.

A thought-provoking role model for our male readers who think they have what it takes to sleep their way to the top is Porfirio "Rubi" Rubirosa, aka the Pepper Grinder. Whereas Pamela was a master technician, a courtesan who knew how to make the most of her assets, Rubi was a natural sexual athlete.

Rubi's wives included the daughter of Rafael Trujillo, president of the Dominican Republic, and two of richest women in the world, tobacco heiress Doris Duke and Woolworth heiress Barbara Hutton. It's not what he received in his divorce settlements that make him special, though he was given a B-25 bomber that had been customized into a flying hotel suite, a seventeenth-century mansion in Paris, and a coffee plantation in the Dominican Republic. What makes Rubi a role model is that while servicing rich women he had the staying power to satisfy an endless list of sex goddesses from Marilyn Monroe to Zsa Zsa Gabor. How did he keep it up, you ask? He had a God-given gift for riding more than just polo ponies and race cars.

To the male readers who have taken off their clothes and looked in the mirror and still think they can follow Rubi's footsteps into the boudoir, know that his popularity with grateful and generous ladies was due in no small part to the fact that his penis was so large it earned him the nickname the Pepper

Grinder, that is, the twenty-four-inch, two-handed model that French waiters to this day still refer to as "Rubirosas." No question, Rubi deserves an asterisk in the record book due to the fact that he climbed so many mountains pre Viagra.

Moral: Social climbing is all about maximizing your human potential.

Note: Gentlemen who think they can sleep their way to the top à la Rubi should also recognize the cruel truth that it is far harder for a man to fake a convincing orgasm than it is for a woman.

Rarer than being blessed with a pepper grinder at birth is the one-in-a-million chance that you will turn out to be the kind of social climber who meets your first Big Fish, falls in love, and has genuinely fantastic sex. But if the dice do happen to roll that way for you, we urge you to ask yourself the question every social climber should consider when they look at the person next to them in bed: "Is this really the best I can do for *me*?"

Social climbers never settle for less than what they deserve.

It's important to add that those readers who do not have or like sex should feel neither left out nor disadvantaged—some of the most successful social climbers are in fact asexual. Not being a slave to your hormones, undistracted by the biological urge to procreate, you will be able to focus your entire mind and body on what's truly important—friends who will enrich your life and lead to friendships that will bring you so much entrée, acceptance, and power in your own right that other people will want to suck up to you.

If romance isn't in the running, you won't be viewed as

competition with straight, gay, bi, lesbian, or transgender Big Fish. And thus, you will be more trusted. Said Big Fish will seek out your unbiased opinion of their boyfriends, girlfriends, potential wives, fiancés, etc. The truly asexual can be objective and serve as an all-purpose beard. How you can take maximum advantage of this trust will be covered in our Networking chapter.

We live in a changing world. Socially ambitious men who provide escort to society women, whose husbands are either dead, away on business, or seeing their mistresses, aka Walkers, were once almost exclusively gay. Today, in a throwback to the times where eunuchs ruled the sultan's harem, the job of Walker is often best filled by the genuinely asexual.

> Everyone makes mistakes; when you wake up next to one, do not panic.

Merely gather your clothes quickly and explain that you'd love to linger but you have to get home and change for an important meeting. Most important, if anyone later asks how your evening with the Big Fish went, leave out the disappointing sexual details and simply say, "He was fantastic!"—Big Fish always appreciate those who provide false advertising.

8

THE SECRETS OF BEING
A GREAT GUEST

As the novice social climber who begins to attend more elaborate and sophisticated social functions, more will be expected of you as a guest than was required at the basic cocktail party. Those rudimentary hit-and-run guerrilla tactics that got you through your first drinks party as a Mountaineer will not be enough to guarantee success at many of the social events you will soon be invited to.

It's okay to get out of an unpromising conversation at a cocktail party with that time-honored excuse, "I have to freshen my drink," but if you use that excuse too often people really will begin to think you have a drinking problem, even if you didn't meet them at one of those AA meetings we told you to go to when you first came to town.

Crass but true, the trajectory of a social climber's ascent is determined by both the quantity and quality of the invitations he or she receives. In other words, you have to be popular, well-liked, and sought-after in spite of the fact you have far less to offer than your host or hostess surmises. Fool them but never yourself. Whether a social climber lives la dolce vita or dies alone depends on likability.

What's more, to truly make your dreams come true, you have to be popular, well-liked, and sought-after not just for a night or a month or even a year; you have to prove your fabulousness 24/7/365 throughout the course of your whole life.

Yes, that's a daunting task, but only if you look at it as a task—envision it as your manifest destiny and it becomes a privilege.

EMPOWERING THOUGHT #14

Social climbing isn't a part-time occupation, it's a calling. You are joining a priesthood where those who've mastered the teachings of this Bible never have to fly commercial again.

While the priest sells faith and some might say superstition, you are selling something real, tangible, something you care about deeply and genuinely believe in—yourself.

For the Mountaineer, being a great guest involves more than simply self-confidence and having great manners. It means learning how to make yourself an asset to any and every social function you attend. You must deport yourself in a way that makes you as essential an ingredient to the party's success as the choice of caterer, or the regiftability of the items in the goodie bag. In short, your host or hostess must be able to count on you to add to the fun of the fete, even when you don't feel fun or their idea of fun is so unbearable, you'd prefer to be sitting in a dentist's chair getting a root canal.

Note: The rules are different if you are a social climbing Big Fish and are in a position to reciprocate, quid pro quo, with lavish star-studded soirees of your own. For those lucky enough to belong in that tax bracket, a different set of rules apply, which will be covered later. For now, suffice to say the rule of thumb is, the more power/money/fame you possess, the more tolerant polite society will be of sulky, boorish, and out-and-out rude behavior.

EMPOWERING THOUGHT #15

A great social climber does not judge the rich and powerful by his or her own standards. In polite society, a Big Fish big enough to weigh in as a Whale who gets caught having sex with a poodle is not a "perv" but an "animal lover."

Is such a double standard fair? Of course not, but when one embraces a life dedicated to upward mobility, one accepts the innate hypocrisy of the twenty-first-century class system. Why? Because it gives the social climber the moral high ground.

Since we do not make the rules, we can feel righteous when

we bend them for personal gain. The trick is to make the most out of Big Fish hospitality without your host or hostess feeling used.

Often being a great guest means that you have to pretend that you are a better person than you are. Fortunately, a little goes a long way.

> Always be the first guest to volunteer to help put out food, serve drinks, clean up that broken glass, especially if there's a maid in the room and you can count on your host or hostess to say, "That's so sweet of you to offer, but the help can take care of that."

And most important of all, always bring a present. Since you don't have enough money to buy them something they really want, make them something. The hand-crafted gift, the present that shows an investment of what is really precious, your time, will mean the most. Naturally, because of your active social life, you do not have time to waste actually making something hand-crafted. We suggest you buy a dozen jelly jars and the paraffin used to seal them—the kind used by foodies who put up preserves. Then, purchase a dozen jars of Smuckers raspberry preserves on sale at Costco. . . . Hand print a label, draw a heart on it, give it to your host or hostess as you walk in the door, tell them you made it according to your grandmother's treasured recipe, and you've set the stage for success.

That will get you in the door and on the right foot, but to cement your place in their hearts, you must learn to master your emotions and facial expressions so that you can seem genuinely happy when you are trapped in a conversation with your hosts' senile parents, even if they are incontinent and hit on you when they call you into the bathroom for help.

Your joie de vivre must never seem calculated. When you volunteer to waste thirty minutes reading a bedtime story to your host's or hostess's six-year-old even though you know he's infested with head lice, your ersatz kindness must seem absolutely sincere and spontaneous. Why? Because then, your host or hostess will feel guilty for taking advantage of you. And the smart social climber knows it is infinitely easier to make maximum use of Big Fish when they are operating under the misperception that they are using you.

That said, it is also important to remember that though you might have partially if not totally misrepresented who and what you are to have gotten invited to the party, you should never think of yourself as a con artist. Instead, imagine yourself as a cat burglar. When you slip away at the end of any event, however grand or humble (not too humble, one hopes), your host or hostess should never suspect that you have left the party with more than you had when you arrived.

Rest assured, every great guest is a good social climber. How can we say that with such certainty? Because being a great guest is too much work to do it for any other reason. And in America, we don't work for free.

Being entertaining doesn't mean that you always have to sing for your supper (though having a bell-like soprano or a classically trained baritone will make you popular at Christmas caroling parties); it does mean your host or hostess can count on you to be charming in the most difficult circumstances.

The great guest/social climber is not the star of the show, nor should you want to be. Leave that role to be played by your host or hostess, or the Big Fish guest of honor. Like a good character actor's, your performance will be judged by your ability to make the headliners of the show look good. Your job is to cover up their faux pas, bungled jokes, and any and all embarrassing performances at the party.

> Be the hero: When a room goes silent because a Big Fish has said something politically incorrect or had an attack of flatulence, come to the rescue, fill in the silent black hole in the conversation with small talk that makes the main attractions seem more interesting, intelligent, witty, and sober than they often are.

Yes, your host or hostess will appreciate your feigned eagerness to chat up sulky children and senile relatives who are off their meds and refuse to stay locked in their rooms. But what will really put your host or hostess in your debt, i.e., empower you and make you the toast of the town, is to become that rare guest who can be counted on to make polite conversation with anyone and everyone, but most especially with that subspecies of difficult guest—individuals we like to refer to as Wild Boar.

As invasive as kudzu, Wild Boar are, sadly, as much a part of the modern social food chain as Swans, Turtles, Big Fish, and Whales. As unpredictable and savage as his namesake, the Wild Boar's instinctive knack for gutting the fun out of any social gathering in a matter of minutes makes him every Big Fish host's or hostess's nightmare, which in turn makes him the great guest's nightmare.

Most, but not all, Wild Boar are Big Fish who morphed into feral swine due to either too much success too soon or not enough too late. Often, but not always, their success makes them think they are blessed with a great sense of humor; they will take perverse pleasure in flexing their clout and insisting on telling jokes designed to offend everyone in the room, including the dog. Many owe their initial Big Fish success to highly developed math, science, or computer skills that they insist on droning on about, especially if they sense you're not sufficiently impressed. These passive-aggressive techno-nerds with cheese-colored teeth often speak softly only to trick you into leaning close so they can paralyze you with an eyelash-curling blast of halitosis.

Wild Boar come in all shapes and sizes, but the most difficult are those who are so drunk, demented, drugged, and/or powerful they don't feel obliged to include nouns or verbs in their sentences but have to be shown a good time because they hold sway over their host's social position, inheritance, or child's college acceptance.

> Of course, not all Wild Boars are native to America. Some are simply French people who insist on speaking French to those who don't speak it.

How does a social climber make polite conversation with bores, fools, and/or French people, especially if you don't speak French?

We call our patent-pending method of surefire shortcuts to el-oquence the Rick James Method of Intelligent Small Talk, in honor of the much-maligned pioneering practitioner of the technique.

Yes, *that* Rick James, the late, great master of funk who gave the world such classics as "Super Freak" and "Give It to Me Baby." *The Social Climber's Bible*'s method of conversation was inspired by Mr. James's ability to carry on polite conversation from dusk to dawn with a dozen different individuals from all walks of life by responding to any and everything that was said to him with the same four-word phrase.

Impossible, you say? Well, here are a few examples of how it worked or, rather, how we were told Mr. James masterfully worked it.

When a record executive broached the subject of dinner, "Is anyone else hungry?" Mr. James responded, "And you *know* that."

Later, when asked, "Should we get some more blow?" Mr. James's response? "And you *know* that."

During dinner, when someone queried, "Is that bitch a really hot chick or a really cute guy?" Mr. James's answer? "And you *know* that."

When politics came up in the conversation and a member of his entourage demanded, "Are you gonna sit there and let Rea-ganomics screw the poor, or are you going to stand up and fucking do something?" Mr. James's response was a sage: "And you *know* that."

In these examples, you can see how Mr. James deftly avoided committing to being for or against anything by always answering with "And you *know* that." He left it up to the people who were doing the talking to determine whether he agreed with them. For the social climber who wants to reap the benefits of becoming a great guest, the task of making polite conversation is twice as complicated as it was for Mr. James. Why? Because you not only have to say nothing that could offend a Big Fish whose politics, tastes, and/or prejudices you know nothing about, you, unlike Rick, also have to sound intelligent and sober while saying nothing that could in any way offend.

Even the veteran social climber knows that trapped, bee-drowning-in-honey feeling that comes when the Big Fish you're trying to impress makes a statement that demands a response, but you have no idea what you should say, or even could say, to keep up your half of the conversation without risk of putting your foot in your mouth.

At a loss for words? Unable to make any sense of what an inebriated Big Fish is talking at you about? Trapped in a conversation with someone who sounds as if he's speaking a foreign language even though he's talking in English? Simply repeat any one of our five all-purpose phrases and you will be able to hold up your end of any conversation.

Here's how it works. Suppose you are at a dinner party seated next to a drunk husband or wife who demands you give your opinion about their ex-husband's/wife's recent infidelity. Not surprisingly, Wild Boars of both sexes often find themselves in this position. For the purpose of this exercise, suppose a heartbroken Wild Boar spouse you're trying to have a civilized conversation with recently came home and discovered his or her husband or wife having sex with their manny. And the jilted

Wild Boar demands of you, in a loud voice, "How would you feel if that happened to you?"

Unfortunately, you *can't* say, "They should be horsewhipped" because you know for a fact that your hostess is sleeping with her manny. The table goes quiet. Some of the guests are curious to hear your opinion. Rival social climbers will be looking forward to your going down in flames. You're hoping the spouse has an alcoholic seizure so you don't have to answer. But instead, the Wild Boar slurs, "So what do you have to say to that, Mr. Nobody from Nowhere?"

Now what do you say? Of course, what you'd like to say is, "Fuck you and the horse you rode in on," but that is not considered polite conversation except in a David Mamet play and will not get you a reputation for being a great guest. Instead, stay calm and repeat the first of our multipurpose phrases with a world-weary sigh, "*Tout le monde mange. . . . Et nous sommes le dîner.*" Then translate as if you can actually speak French, "All the world loves to eat, and we are the dinner." Suddenly, you haven't just put out the fire, you're a sage philosopher.

If you have trouble with French, tell the Boar, "You have to love the game beyond the prize." This one not only makes you seem fair, but also reminds everyone at the table, including the jilted drunk, how important it is to be a good sport in life.

If you want to say something that makes you seem more profound, try, "The dogs bark, but the caravan moves on," and you'll be telling them to shut up and put it behind them in a way that makes you sound like you are a disciple of Khalil Gibran.

Simply suggest, "It is what it is," and everybody'll think you're hipper and younger than you are.

Or, if you feel bold and want to distinguish yourself as both a great guest and a forgiving person, you can redirect the conversation in an even more self-serving direction by reaching across the table, grabbing hold of the jilted Wild Boar's hand, and announcing, "I'm renting a villa in Saint Bart's next season, and you should come down for a visit."

Of course, you are doing nothing of the sort. But "next season" is a long way off. In the meantime, the distraught spouse and everyone else at the table will hear your offer and before you have to make up a story next year about the villa rental falling through at the last minute, you will be inundated with invitations offered by fellow guests hoping to trade a weekend in East Hampton, upstate New York, Cape Cod, or the Berkshires with them for a week-long Caribbean freebie with you.

Prepare yourself for awkward social moments to come by memorizing these aforementioned phrases. Once you master them, try the following sayings in a foreign language and you will add twenty points to your upward mobility IQ.

What to Say When You Don't Know What to Say

Chinese: 它肯定胜过尖棒在眼.

Translation: It sure beats a sharp stick in the eye.

Spanish: *Se trata de los más callados que engañar a usted.*

Translation: The quiet ones fool you.

Russian: **Вы должны будете поговорить с моим адвокатом о том, что**.

Translation: You'll have to talk to my lawyer about that.

German: ***Jeder Faden hat zwei Enden***.

Translation: There are two ends to every string.

Portuguese: ***Eles dizem a mesma coisa sobre o polvo***.

Translation: They say the same thing about the octopus.

And always remember, no matter what language you are speaking, it's not what you say that's important, it's how you say it.

9

BASIC SOCIAL FUNCTIONS AND HOW TO GET THE MOST OUT OF THEM

Whether the invite is engraved on gilt-edged paper and delivered by snail mail or arrives via "paperless post," fledgling social climbers feel a heady mix of both excitement and dread when they accept an invitation to a type of social function they've never attended before.

Relax . . . and count yourself lucky that you're not trying to climb the ladder under the weight of those oppressively strict rules of etiquette that burdened past generations of Mountaineers. Times have changed. Men no longer have to dress for a dinner date, much less pay for their date's dinner; likewise, women today are fortunately free to wear white before Memorial Day and are no longer required to make men feel smart.

EMPOWERING THOUGHT #16

The advice contained in your mother's Emily Post will be as helpful with social intercourse today as douching with Coca-Cola was in preventing pregnancy when your mom was a girl.

It is important to remember that though most of the old-fashioned draconian dictates as to what "is" and "isn't" done can be broken or bent without fear of repercussion or reprisal, there are still a few rules that the Mountaineer must at least appear to adhere to.

The simple fact that you purchased *The Social Climber's Bible* indicates you have enough upward mobility in your DNA to realize that, say, for example, the bold, flamboyant style, manner of dress, and Mountaineering techniques that may help you foul-hook a Big Fish at a costume ball will not make you a hit with the movers and shakers at a bris . . . unless of course it's being held at the Kabbalah Center and Madonna is assisting the mohel.

To get the most out of any social function, the size, purpose, and setting of the event should determine the tactics you employ.

You don't just need a game plan for each and every evening—you need a game plan to fall back on when your game plan fails. And the wise climber has a backup backup plan that does not involve getting bombed.

Think like Carl von Clausewitz, the renowned Prussian military strategist, who stressed the importance of taking tactical advantage of the confusion of the battlefield; the element of uncertainty in all military engagements von Clausewitz referred to as the "fog of war." For the social climber, the fog of war is the confusing mist of fun that clouds most social functions. You must always be ready to improvise, to turn a setback into an advantage, a disappointment into an opportunity. And most important of all, always take advantage of party mayhem and have yourself photographed with any and all Big Fish. Ask strangers to photograph you standing next to somebodies, i.e., Whales and famous people, to make it appear as if you are friends with them. The confusing mist of fun will give you a few moments for an intimate pose before the somebody asks you why you are invading their personal space. These photos will help you seem more popular and better connected than you actually are when you rejoin Facebook.

Of course, sometimes you cannot change the party. Not often, but sometimes you will discover that not even you—with your charm and the Rick James method of intelligent small talk—can make an event as special as you are. But never forget, you owe it to the person you want to become to make the most of every opportunity, even the disappointing ones.

If, for example, you endure a three-hour bus ride to attend a barbecue because you heard the grill master was going to be Warren Buffett and discover that Warren Buffett is indeed flipping the burgers but is not *that* Warren Buffett, don't waste time sulking or chastising yourself. Find out what this Warren Buffett can do for you. Who knows—he might own a shitload of stock in Berkshire Hathaway, or perhaps he's Jimmy "Margaritaville" Buffett's cousin.

Put simply, you won't catch fish if you don't go fishing.

Dinner Parties

There are two types of dinner parties: 1) those where you get to decide where you sit—buffets—and 2) those where your host or hostess tells you where to sit, i.e., the seated dinner.

Given that at your average dinner party you will spend twice as long sitting and eating as you do standing and drinking, who you sit next to will to a large degree determine whether the evening is a success or a failure.

Because the tactics and strategies open to you are vastly different at a buffet versus at a seated dinner, it is of utmost importance that you ascertain as soon as possible after arriving whether the dinner is seated or not.

After you have greeted your hosts, presented them with a jelly jar of what by now is your legendary faux-fruit compote, told them they look fantastic, thanked them for inviting you, and complimented them on their beautiful home/apartment/

child, immediately slip into the dining room, out onto the terrace, into the garden, or wherever the dinner's going to be served. If you see plates stacked on the table rather than places set, you'll know it's a buffet—or the help is very sloppy.

If it is indeed a buffet, you are master or mistress of your own fate in regard to seating. Return to the room where the predinner cocktails are being served and survey the crowd for the most advantageous dinner partner. Calculate the number of guests who are in fact Big Fish, and check for the presence of Swans/Turtles. Remember, Turtles will be harder to spot. Chances are your hosts have thrown this buffet so they can eat their dinner nestled between the biggest of the Big Fish and the Swan.

Since the odds are both your hosts and the biggest of the Big Fish want to sleep with the Swan, either in reality or at the very least in their dreams, the best way for you to turn their threesome into a foursome with you squeezed between them is to employ that age-old technique we call Pimping the Swan.

We are not suggesting you do anything as crass as middle-manning a sexual liaison; simply flatter the Big Fish and/or your host/hostess in a way that will let the Swan know it's worth his/her while being nice to the Big Fish. Because Swans, being gorgeous/sexy, do not have to social climb, i.e., work for their invites, Swans are often startlingly uninformed about who their host/hostess is and/or does and more important, what he/she is in a position to do for a Swan. You are merely providing a public service announcement. Casually mention to the Swan that the

Big Fish is freshly divorced and/or has a beach house next door to Calvin Klein. Nonchalantly let it be known your host/hostess has the last word on who will be the next Swan featured in the advertisements for Chanel, Dior, Pep Boys, or the local Dairy Queen—you get the idea.

Remember that the biggest fish for you might not be the one with the most muscle. For example, if you're a struggling novelist, an editor at a publishing house will be far more helpful to you than the CEO of Bank of America—unless the CEO of Bank of America is so smitten with you over dinner, he/she buys a publishing house and orders it to purchase your book. Which will only happen if, after the dinner party, you have fabulous sex with him/her again and again and again. In short, it's often more advantageous for the social climber who's just starting out to go for the smaller Big Fish who commands the pond you need to conquer before you can proceed to deeper waters.

> Word of caution: Do not immediately attach yourself to the Big Fish you desire too early in the evening: You are a climber, not a case of the crabs.

The one exception to this rule applies to those whose personality type fell into the Velcro-Climber category—the climber who stays so tightly glued to the hip of the Big Fish and appears so deaf, dumb, and blind to his/her obvious efforts to ditch him that the Big Fish, out of sheer exhaustion, gives up and accepts him as a bosom buddy. This is not a method we recommend for the sensitive social climber.

Timing is everything. Unless you are a Velcro-Climber, wait until the tail end of the cocktail hour before latching on to the person you want to sit next to at a buffet. Since Big Fish love to talk about themselves, and you have googled them in the powder room, as you line up for plates and food, ask the Big Fish a question that will require an answer that will allow the Big Fish to brag about at least two of the reasons he or she is so great. For example: "I hear you're both a noted big-game hunter and on the board of PETA."

Time it right, and by the time you both get to the end of the buffet line, the Big Fish will insist on your sitting next to them so they can finish regaling you with how fantastic they are.

Know that you undoubtedly will not be the only social climber on the guest list. If you discover that the Big Fish who can change your life is already being monopolized by some other Mountaineer, it's best to watch and wait. Do not try to break into their conversation or, worse, show your hand by interrupting to ask the Big Fish where they are going to sit and attempt to save a place next to them by placing your jacket/purse/sweater/manbag on a chair or sofa. Why? Because while you're busy saving seats, the competition will get ahead of you in the buffet line with the Big Fish and when you get back with your dinner, they will have tossed your stuff behind the sofa and stolen your seats.

The best method to get the seat you want and deserve at a

buffet dinner is to employ a technique we call the Gracious Hover. When your host/hostess announces dinner is being served, hover in the dining room where the plates and napkins have been put out. Let the non-Keepers, the less-than-delectable potential dinner partners, go ahead of you, handing each one of them a plate. Never miss an opportunity to look as if you have better manners than you actually do.

When the Big Fish you're after gets in line with the social climber who has been monopolizing him or her, carefully step forward, three plates in hand. Offer the first to the Big Fish. Then, deftly slip into line between the Big Fish and the competition, handing the third plate to the rival you just cut off, making it seem as if you are simply trying to be polite. With your back to the climber behind you, it'll be easy for you to exclude him or her from the conversation as you make small talk with the Big Fish about the entrées offered. If you see the Big Fish ask for gluten-free bread, confess that you, too, swing gluten-free. Vegan? Pescatarian? Strictly kosher? What a coincidence, you as well. By the time you get to the end of the line, the Big Fish will be asking you to help him or her ditch the sycophant who's been stalking him or her throughout the cocktail hour.

Of course, if after greeting your host/hostess you duck into the dining room/terrace/garden/wherever and discover a set table with place cards bearing names, none of the above jockeying for position will help you improve your position in the world. Unless, of course, you are a celebrity. Barbara Walters, for example, is said to be notorious for surreptitiously improving her placement, and at one event, Ms. Walters had the admirable nerve to switch the place card of the guest of honor with her own so she could have the honor of sitting next to Hillary Clinton.

Seated dinners pose a challenge to even the most experienced social climber. Particularly if he or she is not seated next to a Big Fish and/or a Swan. But if a climber stays calm and can improvise, the worst seat in the house can become the catbird seat.

If you don't recognize the names of those seated on either side of you, quickly cyberstalk them. If you're a newbie to the dinner party circuit, do not be surprised if the Internet reveals them to be subsomebodies. As a fledgling climber, you are filler. The best you can realistically hope for is that one of the two nobodies who are going to bookend your evening are companions, life partners, significant others, or spouses of a Big Fish, rather than your host or hostess's yoga instructor, personal trainer, or acupuncturist.

You might wonder, why not just ask your host or hostess if the dinner is seated and who you are going to be seated next to when you first arrive? Because that would reveal that you cared about such things. Which is tantamount to admitting you are a social climber. Which, as we established at the start of the book, is the last thing a clever social climber wants to be known as. Hard as it might be to stifle your indignation over subzero seating, fight the urge to openly ask your host or hostess to change your placement. Requesting a different seat at the table, particularly if you ask to be moved to a seat next to a somebody, will show your hand.

If you are desperate, seated between a pair of major Wild Boars, or next to an octogenarian who has forgotten how to swallow his own saliva, the only way to request a seat change that won't put you at a tactical disadvantage for the rest of the evening is to take your host or hostess aside, smolder, and then whisper in their ear, "I was hoping I'd get to sit next to you."

Of course, this move is not without risk. Your host or hostess may interpret your plea as a request for more than you want or is in your best interest to deliver. If you both do in fact have a mutual unsatiated desire to be closer, this is all fine and good. However, if you aren't prepared to follow up such a flirtatious opening move, you could gain a reputation for being a tease.

> Though many Big Fish like a joke, there are two subjects they do not enjoy being teased about: sex and money.

If you discover you've been placed at the ass end of a dinner table, or have been seated at the obviously less desirable table for B guests, or even worse, discarded to a wobbly card table hurriedly set up in the neighboring room with your host or hostess's no-neck monster relatives, do not complain. In fact, make a point of being thrilled by the seat that has been given you.

EMPOWERING THOUGHT #17

Where your host or hostess places you at a
seated dinner party reveals just how little they
think of you and, as such, it is the only honest
barometer a climber has of his or her current
status.

If your host or hostess has made a public pronouncement of
your lowly status by seating you in Siberia, there's only one way
to rectify it. Return to the room where the cocktails are being
served and your host is undoubtedly chatting up the biggest of
Big Fish. Casually but deliberately mention that you almost had
to miss the dinner you now wish you hadn't said yes to. When
they ask why, say that you've just taken an unexpected forty-
eight-hour business trip to Dubai to meet with new investors or
were in LA talking with Lena Dunham and Steven Spielberg
about the film rights to the novel you're writing, or you were
stuck in the South of France inspecting the villa your grandmother just left you . . . in other words, make something up
that can't be proven untrue, that makes you seem so fabulous
your host and the Big Fish will wish they were slated to sit next
to you.

If, after you have tooted your own horn, the host tries to
switch your seat, do not, repeat, do not! give them the satisfaction. Announce that there is nothing you love more than to have
dinner with "new" people. Take your place proudly among the

dregs of the party and proceed to give the impression to one and all that you are having the time of your life. Laugh at jokes that aren't funny, regale the dullards on your left and right with your best stories about childhood adventures you never had with recently deceased celebrities you never met. Not only will the host who snubbed you worry they might have misjudged you, even better they will also worry that they might have offended you, which means you have succeeded in "flipping it."

Yes, you were dealt a bad hand with your placement, but if you play your cards right, by the end of the evening you will have reversed the power dynamic and they will be sucking up to you.

The Dinner Dance
The dinner dance consists of a well-lubricated cocktail hour designed to "loosen up" the guests for a rumba, a dinner with enough wine to make said guests think they actually do do a great rumba, followed by a dance where it readily becomes apparent that not just WASPs but all rich people are rhythmically challenged. Tellingly, the dinner dance is one of the few lasting contributions WASP culture has made to the modern world.

Because of the expense involved in treating seventy-five or more people to drinks, dinner, a parquet dance floor, and a live band or a celebrity DJ, you can be sure that whoever is throwing the bash is a bona fide Big Fish. Unless, of course, the Big Fish is throwing the party to convince other, even bigger fish that they are more financially solvent than they in fact are so they can borrow money from the bigger fish before they have to declare bankruptcy. Either way, the social climber can count on an abundance of Big Fish, several Turtles, at least one Swan, and perhaps a genuine Whale. This is the kind of pond you want to fish in!

Your invitation will usually indicate what you're expected to wear:

> For a man, Black Tie means what was once politely called a "dinner suit"—and vulgarly referred to as a "Tux." Women are expected to know that for them Black Tie translates as a dress no one has seen you in.

In recent years, it has become increasingly and annoyingly common to receive dinner dance invitations that merely stipulate "Festive Dress"—an attire designation that is both confusing and culturally insensitive. If you are a member of a South American indigenous tribe, be forewarned: Festive Dress does not mean showing up festooned in parrot feathers and an ancestral penis sheath, though if you have the body for it, that is undeniably a great conversation starter.

What Festive Dress really means is that your hostess has a killer couture ensemble she is dying to wear and wants to make sure she cuts a better figure than you by tricking you into wearing something that will make you look foolish and underdressed in comparison. Those who followed our advice in Chapter 1 and have used a sartorial statement (turban/sari/kilt, etc.) to define themselves should not break character. If you haven't, play it safe and wear something that makes you look simply elegant and far richer than you are. How do you do that? If your closet doesn't contain evening wear, know that every rich zip code has at least one charity thrift shop. Purchase a secondhand tux or festive gown that's thirty years out of fashion and casually mention your grandfather/grandmother wore it to the White House.

Because dinner dances are ninety-nine times out of a hundred seated affairs, the social climber will once again find they are at the mercy of their host. However, if the dinner dance is particularly large or the dinner tables are set up in a separate location that is slightly removed from the area where the cocktail hour takes place, you do have other options.

If you hate the seat you've been assigned and you're not at the host's table, you can get away with exchanging your place card with that of someone who has better dinner partners. But be careful. It's a bold move. And know that if you hope to get away with it, you have to not only change the placement of your name card, but also change the seating of at least two other tables—twenty other people—to make sure you are not immediately suspected.

EMPOWERING THOUGHT #18

Switching your place card at a seated event is not bad manners. Getting caught switching your place card at a seated event is bad manners.

If logistics or the presence of a sharp-eyed party planner or major domo of a Big Fish make it impossible for you to rearrange the seating on the sly, do not be dejected. Your dinner table obligations at a dinner dance are more relaxed than those at a small dinner party. Yes, you still have to make polite conversation with the people on your left and right for a minimum of five minutes, but after that, as soon as the band begins to play and couples take to the dance floor, you can and should escape.

Unlike those given favorable placement at an A list table, you will be free to ditch the dullards you've been stuck with and get a head start table-hopping. When you pop into an empty seat vacated by a couple who've left for the dance floor at a table of Big Fish, you'll not only be able to take over the conversation— you can drink their wine and eat their lamb chops before they get back to the table.

Now, old-school sticklers will tell us that every male guest should ask every woman at the table to dance at least once. Remember this: Most seating is arranged boy-girl. And since most tables seat ten, that's five dances, i.e., too much time to waste, especially if you've gotten a bum seat to begin with.

Today, a man isn't obligated to dance with anyone. But he will seem more suave than he is and be more likely to be invited to the next big party if he takes his hostess for a spin around the dance floor. If you are suave but do not know how to dance, consult YouTube; mastering the rudiments of the Dougie, Sprinkler, and Electric Slide will get you on and off the dance floor without breaking one of her toes.

> If you do injure your hostess while dancing, particularly if she begins to bleed, quickly tap the nearest male on the shoulder and say, "I think you owe our hostess an apology."

Regrettably, the dancing element at dinner dances does not afford the female social climber the same opportunities for advancement as it does male Mountaineers. If a female social climber of average looks asks a male Big Fish, particularly if he is slightly inebriated, to dance, he is going to make the deluded assumption that she is interested in his body rather than what he can do for her.

Costume Parties

Though your average social climber is likely to receive only one or two invites per year that stipulate costume and/or theme (that is, unless you're a drag queen), we focus on this subspecies of fete because the costume party, what the English call "fancy dress," offers the Mountaineer opportunities not found at any other social function.

For example, if you see Lloyd Blankfein, CEO of Goldman Sachs, or Janet Yellen, chair of the Federal Reserve, at a cocktail party wearing a business suit, you are going to be intimidated. But if Lloyd or Janet or someone else with their kind of juice is at a costume party dressed as, say, a Care Bear, he or she is not only approachable but huggable. Putting on a costume lowers the defenses of a Big Fish or Whale. More important, it empowers you. Why? Because Big Fish and Whales aren't used to feeling foolish. Whereas you are.

Big Fish costumed as Napoléon, Joan of Arc, Caligula, et al., will subconsciously worry that they have revealed something they've worked hard to keep hidden their whole lives: their true nature. While you, no matter what costume you're wearing, know exactly who and what you are—a Mountaineer.

While everybody knows what Lloyd Blankfein is, even when he is in costume, you are still a mysterious and unknown quantity.

The real advantage you get from wearing a mask and fancy dress to a costume party is that it allows you to find out just where you stand on the ladder. Say your name is Sally Powers. If you are costumed and masked at a party and happen upon a group of guests who have not met you but know people who you met through social climbing, join the conversation and casually volunteer, "I hear Sally Powers is an incredibly smart gal."

If they nod in agreement and say, "That's what all my friends say about Sally," you'll know you're on the road to success. If they snicker or worse, laugh, or even worse, tell you, "My buddy says Sally Powers is the worst social climber he's ever met," you will know you still have work to do and should immediately go home and reread the preceding chapters.

EMPOWERING THOUGHT #19

Costume parties, particularly those held on Halloween, are thrown with the understanding

> that revelers of either sex who arrive in
> garter belts, Speedos, fishnet stockings, high
> heels, leather chaps—i.e., the slutty nurse, the
> slutty fireman, the slutty schoolgirl, the slutty
> cowboy—are not actually slutty people but
> merely people masquerading as sluts.

Now, if you dressed that way and went to a normal party and danced provocatively around a Big Fish or Whale, the assumption would be that you are a slutty hooker intent on exchanging sex for money and/or services provided by the Big Fish. But on Halloween, social climbers who want to see what it's like to sleep their way to success can try trick-or-treating with a Big Fish or better yet, a Whale, without fear of waking up in the morning feeling guilty that they have in fact just become a slutty prostitute.

Charity Balls and Benefits

Charity galas are basically dinner dances put on to raise money for a good cause. They come in all shapes and sizes. Some benefit endangered species, others help starving children. But even if they are raising money to provide sex toys to the homeless, your job is to make sure the charity gala you're attending benefits you as much as whatever good cause it's being thrown for.

But if you are young or a financially challenged social climber, and a Big Fish invites you to a benefit, be careful. Before saying yes to attending any charity function, it is important for you to ascertain whether the Big Fish is inviting you to be a guest for the evening or inviting you to have the privilege of purchasing a thousand-dollar ticket. Do-gooder Big Fish are often cunning, if not downright dishonest, in how they offer invitations to charity events. They will make it seem as if they want you for your youth, beauty, vitality, fresh ideas, and witty repartee and then send you two tickets to something you don't really want to go to and, after the party's over, hit you up with a bill you can't afford to pay.

To avoid any embarrassing misunderstanding or trap laid by the unscrupulous Big Fish fund-raiser, always say, "I'd love to be your guest, but there's a good chance I will have to fly to Burma that night." When the formal invitation arrives with a bill, you will have a ready-made excuse.

EMPOWERING THOUGHT #20

Do *not* feel guilty about *not* purchasing tickets to charity events you can't afford (especially if you did not pocket the money you collected for UNICEF trick-or-treating as a child); you must never forget that the "pleasure of your company" is the most generous donation a good social climber can make to any event. Your sense of self-worth should not allow you to pay other people for the privilege of your presence at their party.

Since rock stars and Academy Award–winning actors who attend charity events don't have to pay for their tickets, why should you? If after you have emailed the Big Fish that you unfortunately cannot attend due to your imaginary business trip to Burma, they persist in trying to get you to make a donation, give them a demotion . . . in your contacts. A Big Fish who asks a social climber for money is not only a bad judge of character, they are a non-Keeper and, most important, not a true Big Fish.

Those Mountaineers with the financial wherewithal to pay for a charitable climb, who can afford to cough up the hundred thousand dollars it takes to buy a table at the Metropolitan Museum's annual gala or the Save Venice ball or Elton John's amfAR benefit, should consult Advanced Social Climbing for a detailed analysis of what kind of entrée they're really getting for their money.

EMPOWERING THOUGHT #21

If you're a fledgling social climber and a Big Fish invites you to sit at a table at a charity event that costs them tens of thousands of dollars, chances are your Big Fish host doesn't have that many socially acceptable friends; ergo your Big Fish might not be socially acceptable.

If your Big Fish has to resort to you to fill the seats they can't sell, it is more than likely that you are going to be in the company of the newly minted Big Fish's employees, lame relatives, or social climbers even lower on the ladder than yourself.

> If you find yourself at a less-than-stellar table at a stellar event, it is important for you to spend enough time away from the table to make it seem to others at the event that you aren't sitting at a table with the nouveau Big Fish and his tacky friends. We are not suggesting that you ignore your B list Big Fish host, merely that you treat him and your tablemates to intense bursts of your charm before making up a series of excuses that will allow you to escape the contagion of being perceived as his guest.

Generally, you will be fairly judged "rude" if you leave the table more than ten minutes before dessert is served. Vary the excuses you use to escape. If you keep saying you have to go to the bathroom, they will suspect you of having a spastic colon or a drug habit. It's best to space your departures. Five minutes after sitting down and telling one short, hilarious anecdote, announce that you forgot to wash your hands. By the time you return to your table, the first course will be there. After a second brief, funny story, apologize for having to excuse yourself yet again, this time to make a phone call to a sick relative or to check on a business deal. When you return, look exasperated. Why? The line was busy. Remember to always make it seem that there is nothing you would rather do than remain in your seat and enjoy their second-rate hospitality.

What do you do when you are not going to the bathroom and not placing calls to nonexistent sick relatives? Once you are a discreet distance from the table where you're actually sitting, walk purposefully through the ballroom, as if you're looking for someone (i.e., employ the convincing cocktail party wave to a somebody across the room whom you've never met). It's important that more substantial Big Fish see you and make the erroneous assumption that you paid thousands for a ticket and have friends there to wave to.

If anyone asks why you're sitting with Mr. B-level Big Fish, simply say that you bought your ticket at the last minute, and because the charity means so much to you, you told the committee you didn't care where you sat.

If you feel bold and want to hop to the table of a really Big Fish but do not know anyone at that table and have never met Mr. A-plus Big Fish, do not be shy. Simply approach the Big Fish confidently, shake his or her hand, and introduce yourself by saying, "Your support means so much to us, I want to personally thank you for coming." The Big Fish will immediately think you're on the committee that's throwing the ball. Never miss an opportunity to spark a rumor about yourself that makes you look like a great person.

Funerals and Wakes

Funerals other than your own are a great place to social climb.

Yes, you will be sad when the Big Fish you've worked so hard to get to know suddenly dies on you. But don't let grief keep you from making the most of their funeral. Besides the fact that "life belongs to the living," and the thousands of other clichés about the inevitability of death are all true, if your dead Big Fish was really your friend and cared about you, they would want you to get more out of the graveside service than a cold.

If the Big Fish parents or grandparents of a casual acquaintance pass away, don't just call the semistranger on the phone or email your condolences. Knock on their door, bring them a jar of your famous "homemade" preserves. Even if you don't know them very well and never met their deceased relative, be there for them, i.e., hug strangers who start to cry, and gracefully make sure you're invited to all social functions involving the funeral. By respectfully listening as calls go out to Big Fish friends of the deceased, you will be able to ascertain if it's a funeral worth driving across town for versus one that merits a cross-state drive.

Wakes are basically cocktail parties with tears. Mountaineers of all ages will discover that grief, death, and being reminded of just how little time we have at this earthly party called life has a curious effect on Big Fish and Whales—it makes them wonder who will come to their funeral. Knowing that they've had to be a dick to a great many people in the course of becoming a somebody, and that one day soon they will be lying in state at their own bon voyage party, the Big Fish/Whale will begin to worry about the prospect of empty pews at their own funeral. Faced with their own mortality, they will be open to making friends with someone like you.

> You are not taking advantage of grief-stricken Big Fish by becoming their new best friend at the funeral, you're offering them solace. Yes, they probably will be more inclined to say yes when you ask if you could stop by their office and get them involved in a "good cause," i.e., your search for gainful employment. But also know that you may be their last opportunity for redemption.

If you are a young social climber, remember that your youth and vitality will be a comfort to middle-aged Big Fish at a funeral. Why? Because when they look at you, they'll be able to forget that sad fact that they are already on the back nine of their eighteen.

Pretend to be riveted when an oldie Big Fish bores you with stories about how he and the deceased cheated to win a club championship or made their first million cornering the tapioca market.

> Funerals are a great time for making the snob feel guilty about being a snob.

Even if they have snubbed you in the past or failed to return your phone calls, or even if they reported you to the police for texting nude photos of yourself to their son or daughter, forgive them, hug them, tell them they remind you of your mother or father. With the Grim Reaper so close at hand, they will be inclined to consider the possibility that they just might get a better deal on the Other Side if they do something nice to somebody as unimportant as yourself.

The Weekend

Generally speaking, people who can help you have second homes, and people who have third, fourth, and fifth homes can help you even more. Whether their nonprimary weekend residence is a place in the country, a house on the beach, or a ski chalet in the mountains, if you have followed our advice at the social functions we have covered, you will soon be receiving an invitation to spend the weekend with a Big Fish. Though your Big Fish host or hostess will assure you that your thirty-six- to forty-eight-hour stay in their domain will be totally relaxed, it won't be for you unless you remember the following.

Expect the best, but plan for the worst. Your idea of "casual" might be cutoffs and flip-flops, but your hostess might interpret the word to mean your Bermuda shorts don't have to have a crease in them. Similarly, you might be surprised to find that a Big Fish who says the weekend will be "do your own thing" actually means he or she is a swinger, and wearing a bathing suit would be considered bad manners. Learn how to read between the lines of the invitation, and know that invariably, if your host or hostess describes the weekend to come as "nothing fancy," it almost always is, i.e., bring your jacket and tie or a cocktail dress.

To get an idea what you're in for, what you need to bring besides your charm, and how you can get the most out of your stay, it's always best after saying "yes" and "sounds fantastic/ beautiful" to add "do you have any pictures of your place?"

If their "camp" is in fact a twenty-eight-room cottage once owned by a meat-packing heir, L.L. Bean won't cut it. If they don't have any photos of their weekend retreat on their iPhone, Google Earth it in their presence on your cellphone. As you focus in on the satellite pic of their piece of heaven, linger on the neighboring properties. If they are owned by other Big Fish, your host or hostess won't hesitate to tell you so. Knowing what other Big Fish are in the neighborhood, and where they reside, is absolutely essential if you want to get the most out of the weekend, given that you have to know where they live if you are going to pop in on them and make their acquaintance. How are you going to do that? Read on.

Nine times out of ten, Big Fish have multiple homes, not just because they love the country air or adore the beach; what they love is showing off the fact that they are Big Fish. The second-third-fourth home validates their status. The bigger the house, the bigger the fish—unless you have been invited to spend the weekend with the old-money New England variety of Big Fish who take perverse pride in the lack of luxury offered by their homes and enjoy making themselves and their guests uncomfortable.

The barb in this method of Big Fish validation is that monster houses have many bedrooms. And if those bedrooms are unoccupied by guests for more than two weekends in a row, the Big Fish will start to wonder, *Is there something wrong with me*? Or worse, *Is there something wrong with my house*? Or both? Which of course leads to a troubling, existential question that is anathema to all Big Fish—*Could it be being a Big Fish isn't all it's cracked up to be?* All of which often prompts them to invite someone they know little or nothing about and isn't even sure they like to be a guest for the weekend, i.e., you.

EMPOWERING THOUGHT #22

Big Fish may enjoy sitting by themselves admiring the sunset behind their three hundred acres of forested mountaintop or feel good about not having to share their private stretch of waterfront with another living soul, but what brings them the most pleasure is sharing the privileges of their lifestyle with someone they know desperately wants what they have but cannot afford it.

The social climber's and the Big Fish's weekend dreams are interdependent, particularly in the dog days of summer—just as the struggling Mountaineer with the broken AC unit is desperate to get invited out of the city, the Big Fish with the big beach houses feel an urgency to fill their guests rooms so they don't feel like losers. Always remember, they need you as much as if not more than you need them.

The Big Fish's reasons for wanting a guest for the weekend are twofold: Validation of their enviability plays into the equation, but much of their desire to have the pleasure of your company simply stems from what Big Fish often refer to when talking to their shrinks as ennui, aka what a poor person would call boredom.

Know that Big Fish couples, especially those who have been married for a number of years, even those who seem glamorous and have fun on the party pages of glossy magazines, invariably and inevitably run out of both nice and not nice things to say to each other and need a guest to break the deafening silence of the weekend.

The Duke and Duchess of Windsor (ex-king Edward and Wallis Simpson) were so desperately bored with each other after a few years of marriage they would sit in restaurants reciting the alphabet so it would appear they still had something to say to each other. The duke and duchess were also such status guests they were able to charge American Big Fish who wanted to brag about having royal company for the weekend—according to one well-known society hostess, the guest rate was a thousand dollars a night. The check made out to that amount was to be left in the duchess's lingerie drawer. Though you are not in the same league as the Duchess of Windsor—inarguably one of the greatest social climbers of the twentieth century—you, like the duchess, should know the value of your company.

Sometimes you will be included in the weekend not simply to entertain your host and hostess but to jolly along a particularly difficult but important guest, i.e., the Wild Boar your host and hostess can't bear to spend time with. The specific reasons for inclusion in the weekend will vary, but as with the dinner party, the social climber's responsibility is to make the weekend fun, even if it isn't fun.

Because being fun for forty-eight hours is exhausting, even if your host or hostess is supplying you with drugs, you must remember to pace yourself. Remember, it is hard to cut a good figure if cocaine leads to a bloody nose, and cardiac arrest is a total fun killer.

If the Big Fish, when offering the invitation, inquires if you play golf and/or tennis, know that if you say yes, he will get you up at dawn and drag you to on the links/court as often as he thinks it's fun to play, not necessarily as often as you think it's fun to play. More important, do not admit to playing golf, tennis, bridge, backgammon, badminton, or any other variety of fun where there is a winner and loser unless you not only play well enough to let the Big Fish win without making it obvious you're throwing the match to curry favor, but also have the gamesmanship to guarantee that if teamed up with him in a game of doubles and/or in a foursome of golf, you have the skills to ensure victory.

Generally, the Great Weekend Guest is expected to be a gracious loser when playing any games where score is kept with his or her host.

Being a good loser and making polite conversation through three meals a day are just part of what is expected of a great guest. You also have to say yes to whatever activities or pastimes the Big Fish thinks of as de rigueur for a weekend to qualify as "great," i.e., touch football on the beach with the Big Fish and his son who plays middle linebacker at Stanford and likes to hurt you, the eight-mile jog through the bear-infested woods, or being forced to swim to the lighthouse through a school of jellyfish, etc., etc., etc. All of which is exhausting. And if there's a Wild Boar in the house, it will be doubly exhausting. Think of the weekend not as a marathon but as a series of social climbing sprints.

You will need time alone between events to recharge your batteries and regain your sanity if you want to be at your best at dinner. How does a great guest escape his or her host or hostess for a few hours without seeming rude?

Here are a few excuses that have worked well for us. Announce when you first arrive on Friday that despite your reputation as a bon vivant, devil-may-care kind of guy or girl, you are in fact deeply religious, and hope that they will understand if you take an hour or two off to drive yourself to the nearest synagogue, church, or mosque. If you are in a part of the country that has no minarets, steeples, or enough fellow Jews to form a minyan, you're still in luck if you're a Muslim, because you can simply retreat to your bedroom five times a day and pray to Mecca.

For those social climbers who are known atheists, we suggest that when you first receive your invitation for the weekend, you reveal to your host or hostess that a relative of yours is buried in the local cemetery and that you hope they wouldn't mind if you skipped away for a few hours to visit the grave. Big Fish rarely like to visit cemeteries for the simple reason that they don't like to consider the possibility that the world could go on without them.

What do you do while your Big Fish host or hostess thinks

you are attending religious services or visiting the cemetery where your relative is not buried? Look for better opportunities to climb.

Slip a pair of binoculars and a bird book in your pocket. Drive/bike/walk far enough from the Big Fish's weekend retreat that you cannot be observed by the Big Fish or any of their equally exhausting guests or relatives. Now wander onto the property that belongs to the Big Fish your host or hostess bragged about when you Google-mapped the village where they own their second home.

If these neighboring Big Fish you've never met but would like to get to know ask you why you are trespassing, pull out your binoculars and bird book. Inform them that you stumbled onto their property by accident while you were "birding." Seem excited, look up into the branches of the trees, or point to a stretch of beach grass and whisper, "I've just spotted an Acadian flycatcher (or a piping plover)." Whatever species you choose, just make sure it's "endangered." Yes, there is the small risk that the Big Fish might actually call the police or sic their rottweilers on you, but you will discover most Big Fish homeowners will be immensely pleased to learn an endangered species was spotted on their property because it will give them another thing to brag about.

A word of caution: Do not immediately volunteer the name of the Big Fish you are spending the weekend with. Chances are that they if they were friends with the Big Fish you're staying with, your host would have mentioned the fact and invited them over for dinner, lunch, or touch football with the son who likes to hurt people. Hence, it is prudent to merely say that you first spotted the endangered species of bird over by the house of the

Big Fish where you are spending the weekend. Now, if the Big Fish you've just introduced yourself to announces, "Those ghastly people?" it is wise not to mention the fact that you are staying with them. However, if the Big Fish says, "That's my cousin Bill," of course reveal that you're Cousin Bill's guest, but also add that you can't stay and talk anymore about piping plovers or endangered flycatchers because you're late for church or synagogue, or have a date with a dead relative at a local graveyard.

Every social climber, even if they are the greatest of guests, sometimes finds him- or herself trapped in a hell weekend: *Rain* and sharing a double bed with a fellow climber who snores. *Rain* and an infestation of bedbugs. *Rain* and a couple with three children under the age of four whose nanny has just quit, etc. Big Fish being Big Fish, your host will of course be offended by and suspicious of any attempt to cut a *Rain* weekend short, except of course if you give them a reason to want you to leave early.

If the nearest pharmacy is an hour's drive away, announcing that you left your antiseizure medication back in the city will usually suffice—they will not want to drive you to the pharmacy, and, seizures often being messy due to a loss of bladder control, they will be happy to let you go home early. Feign a back injury that requires them to carry you to and from the toilet and they will not protest when you volunteer to depart ahead of schedule. If the Big Fish has small children, announce you've recently been exposed to dengue fever, and they will force you to leave early.

For the single social climber, it's worth pointing out that the most difficult weekends are often those where your Big Fish host or hostess has forgotten to mention that they have invited you out to the country/beach/mountains because they want to set you up with someone who doesn't meet your standards in the looks/status/fame/fortune/charm/oral-hygiene department.

Because the loser will have invariably been told by your host or hostess that you like his/her type, know that he/she will insist on accompanying you if you try to escape to a religious service or visit the graveyard. If your host or hostess is too big a fish to offend and leaving early is out of the question, your best bet is to limit your unwanted suitor's mobility early in the weekend. Volunteer to help in the kitchen, and drop a Crock-Pot full of hot beef bourguignon in his/her lap. Accidentally on purpose let your nine iron or tennis racquet collide with a part of his/her body that will not do permanent damage but will keep him/her off the beach and out of your hair until you depart on Sunday.

Last but not least, if you are a weekend guest where there is staff, always remember to tip the maid who cleans the room. Why? Because maids are usually locals. And locals gossip, i.e., there is an excellent chance he or she knows you weren't attending church or synagogue or retreating to your room to pray to Mecca. Fifty dollars is the customary cost of purchasing domestic silence in regard to any misbehavior that does not involve the maid's perjuring herself in a court of law.

Note: If you are a social climber who is sleeping your way to the top and you have surreptitiously bedded down with the Big Fish's spouse and/or a guest other than the one you've been set up with, the maid will know and fifty dollars will not be enough.

Thank-You Notes

If you have been invited to any of the social functions previously mentioned, you will need to write a thank-you note. Or in the case of the funeral, a letter of condolence. Which is in essence a sad thank-you note. We are old-school when it comes to written thank-yous. Not because we are slaves to outmoded social conventions, but because the handwritten thank-you posted in the mail is the most cost- and time-effective gesture a social climber can make to ensure he or she is invited back.

> Emailed thank-you notes send a subliminal message that you think your host or hostess isn't worth a fifty-cent stamp and a walk to the mailbox. Texted thank-yous such as "tks 4 aweso w/ end" will give your host or hostess the impression that you don't know how to spell. And tweeted thank-yous, however widely circulated, will imply that your gratitude is limited to 140 characters.

> Thank-you notes should be written in ink by hand.

Younger readers who have become so dependent on keyboards and T-9 that they now point with their thumbs and find writing difficult should invest in a fountain pen and take a calligraphy course. Google Noël Coward. We don't expect you to be able to write like him, but with a little practice, you can print like him.

In the ill-mannered age we live in, composing a handwritten thank-you note is as impressive as the composition of a sonnet was in Shakespeare's time. It is both quaint and formal, especially if written on expensive stationery that includes a nonexistent family crest or is embossed with the silhouette of that stately home your family has, unfortunately, never owned.

EMPOWERING THOUGHT #23

A well-written thank-you note, providing that it has no spelling errors, will make you seem better bred than you are.

Those of you who have never written or received a thank-you note, use the template below. Substitute the fawning adjectives and appropriate nouns in our all-purpose thank-you and you will seem better-mannered, more eloquent, and more grateful than you probably are.

> Dear _____ (Always use a nickname.)
>   Your _____ will always be _____ to me.
> You are truly_____. The _____ and _____
> were inspirational. I had no idea you possessed
> such _____; so many _____. My _____ is still sore
> from the _____ you _____, and I can still taste the
> _____ of your _____(s). Your generosity _____ me. I
> can't wait to _____ you again.
>   I must _____ you, _____ and _____.
>
>   Best _____ ever,
>
>   _____

(If you crashed the party you are thanking your host for, it is best to include your last name. Why? Because if your thank-you note is charming enough, they'll want to invite you to their next party.)

PS: Your secret is totally safe with me.

(This will guarantee future contact regardless of whether there was a secret told and especially if drugs and/or alcohol were consumed during the event. Your host, uncertain of exactly what they said, will be inclined to solve the mystery of any possible indiscretion on their part by immediately calling you up and inadvertently revealing a secret they hadn't actually revealed. Now they will be forced to invite you back because they know if they don't keep sucking up to you, you will reveal the indiscretion. Knowledge is power.)

10

HANDLING HORMONALLY CHARGED EVENTS: ENGAGEMENT PARTIES AND WEDDINGS

We have devoted a separate chapter to engagement parties and weddings, because these hormonally charged events present Mountaineers with opportunities and challenges not found at other social functions. While love and marriage never did go together like a horse and carriage, we at *The Social Climber's Bible* are happy to report that weddings and social climbing are still inexorably intertwined.

Know that you are not just going to a party where people throw rice, catch bouquets, and cry because they are happy. You are attending a sacred event. A pageant based on traditions designed, choreographed, and costumed so that when coupled with alcohol, those witnessing the spectacle will be prone to succumb to a form of mass delusion and magical forgetting that blinds them to the realities of modern-day nuptials, i.e., that statistics prove that there is a better than 50 percent chance the couple who just promised to love, honor, and obey each other in sickness and in health till death do them part will soon be fighting over the wedding presents in divorce court.

> The same romantic wedding fantasies that inspire normally level-headed, intelligent wedding guests to repress the fact that the virginal bride in white has a live-stream sex show on the Web (which they themselves frequent) and/or ignore the rumors that the dashing groom is still on Grindr will inspire them to "forget" any and all of the less-than-flattering things they have heard about you.

What's important for Mountaineers to know is that this magical forgetting also prompts individuals who would normally spot you as a climber a mile off to fall under the delusion that you are a person of sterling character whom they should do something to help.

But before you can capitalize on the tactical advantages weddings provide the climber, you must first, of course, get invited to the wedding. Which brings us to the subject of:

Engagement Parties

Note: Mountaineers who have been invited to the engagement party because they are the ones getting married should immediately flip ahead to the following chapter, Dating, Love, and Marriage, and find out how to make the most of the social climbing opportunities when you're marrying up.

For those of you who are single and fancy-free, your first job at the engagement party is to do whatever it takes to make sure that you will be invited to the wedding. Know that in these financially uncertain times, you may be worth cocktails and pigs in a blanket but might not be deemed worthy of a three-course meal and a Dom Perignon fountain, especially if they know you can't afford to buy any of the wedding gifts they have registered for at Tiffany's. As with all social functions, you can increase your chances of making the cut if you plan ahead.

The social climber should always be the one to organize a group of the bride's or groom's friends to each donate fifty to one hundred dollars so they can get the betrothed couple a special present. Volunteer not only to collect the money but also to make the purchase with *your* credit card. We don't suggest you do anything as crass as claiming to have paid for this present entirely by yourself. Simply forget to include the gift card that lists the names of those who contributed and accidentally leave your credit card receipt in the box that contains the present, and the bride and groom will assume you paid for it by yourself.

A great present will get you off on the right foot at the engagement party. But to actually secure an invite to the wedding, you will also have to make a great impression. And to do that, you must navigate the undercurrent of anxiety that is ever present at all engagement parties due to the fact that there's no guarantee that the engagement party will be followed by a wedding party. And as such, the engagement will turn out to be both a waste of money and a social embarrassment. Usually, whoever's paying for the party is "the party" that most wants the marriage to go through, i.e., either the bride is pregnant or one of the betrothed's parents hopes for financial gain before the balloon payment on their mortgage comes due.

The high hopes, higher stakes, and uncertain outcome of engagements kindles a giddy sexual energy that prompts some to make the mistake of offering a toast that references the future bride's or groom's previous romantic indiscretions. Resist the temptation to turn the engagement party into a roast. The mother of the future bride will not feel inclined to send you an invitation to the wedding if you raise your glass to wish them well by offering up an anecdote that includes the details of her daughter's or future son-in-law's first ménage à trois, especially if it involved you. Play it safe and get off on a good foot by deliberately mistaking the bride's or groom's mother for her or his older sister.

If you want to sleep with the bridesmaids or groomsmen at the wedding, do not sleep with them at the engagement party. Think of the engagement party as a research trip. Say you have only just met the betrothed and you've gotten yourself invited to the engagement party because you heard the wedding's going to be held in a château in Uzbekistan; sounds great. The only trouble is that in certain parts of Uzbekistan, a château is simply a home where the donkey doesn't sleep in your bedroom.

Likewise, it is prudent to discreetly find out what kind of presents the bride and groom plan to give their attendants before you start lobbying to be picked as maid of honor/bridesmaid/best man/groomsman. Obviously, paying hundreds of dollars for a bridesmaid's dress that's designed to make you look fat and the bride look thin is a good investment if the bride's father is going to give you diamond clips from Tiffany's. But agreeing to rent a cutaway and springing for strippers at a bachelor party is a decidedly bad investment in return for a ceramic beer mug with the date of the wedding hand-painted on it by the groom's mother.

If you are a friend of the bride and upon arriving at the engagement party discover that the groom's family and friends have infinitely more to offer you in terms of connections, future invites, and better vacation homes, this is the time to change your alliances and become the groom's new best friend. If you find yourself thinking, *I would get more out of this fascinating clan if I were the bride- or groom-to-be*, do not hit on the future bride or groom at the engagement party. Wait until they begin to argue about china patterns and prenuptial agreements before telling them that they seem unhappy and volunteering to give them a backrub to help them relax.

> In our view, it is perfectly socially acceptable to steal your friend's fiancé *if you do so* before the wedding invitations have been mailed.

The engagement party isn't always a win-win affair for the betrothed, but it can be for you. Except, of course, if one of the two people getting engaged is your Swan. Once a Swan says "I do" to someone other than yourself, he or she is no longer *your* Swan but becomes someone else's ride to the top.

Yes, being a caring person, you want to see your Swan happy. But are you going to be happy if she brings her fiancé instead of you to all those swell parties? Sure, she will let you tag along at first, but after the wedding, how much love will be left for you? You care about your Swan—are you going to stand by and let her be used by someone other than yourself?

For the social climber in danger of losing his or her Swan, the engagement party is an opportunity to regain control. Yes, you should have nipped the relationship in the bud long before it reached this point, but do not waste time berating yourself. There is still time to do what is best for you.

Swans, being fabulously beautiful and perennially sexy, often get engaged and dis-engaged twice a year (about as often as a real swan molts its feathers). Ultimately, unlike real swans, human Swans rarely mate for life, but between the ages of twenty-eight and thirty-five, they are prone to bouts of magical thinking in which they will delude themselves into believing they are like real swans in that regard. Supplying them with grim statistics that prove that Swan marriages to mere mortals often end in the worst kind of divorce (no alimony) will not convince your average Swan to call off the engagement at the engagement party.

What the smart social climber needs to do is to get the Swan's fiancé to call off the engagement. We are not suggesting you do anything as cruel as actually telling the Swan's fiancé that he is making a grave error, marrying a creature as innately and incurably flighty as a Swan. Your Swan would never forgive you for that. Let someone else plant the seeds of doubt. You will simply water them.

Who could you get to do something as socially unforgivable as sabotaging a couple's engagement at their engagement party?

Because Swans are promiscuous by nature, they can't resist inviting old boyfriends or girlfriends to their engagement parties. Old boyfriends or girlfriends are prone to become intoxicated at the sight of a Swan they once dallied with getting engaged to someone other than themselves, which makes them your perfect accomplice.

After helping the brokenhearted ex to his third, fourth, and fifth shot of tequila, it will be easy for a silver-tongued devil like yourself to talk him into standing up and making a toast in which he will recount one of his many funny misadventures with the Swan. All Swans, being Holly Golightly creatures regardless of sex, have past life experiences they have not shared with their fiancés. The stories you want to convince the drunken ex-boyfriend (or girlfriend) to reveal in the toast might include the transmission of STDs, past drug arrests, or witty anecdotes about how the Swan got crabs in his or her eyelashes.

Remember to quiet the crowd so that not only the unsuspecting Swan's fiancé but the hard-of-hearing parents or grandparents will catch every word. When jaws drop and the room goes quiet, you should be the first one to stand up, turn on the drunken ex-boyfriend or -girlfriend, and take offense. Better yet, help the confused and humiliated fiancé throw the offending ex out the door. Then, pull the fiancé you are actually trying to dispose of and his parents into another room and say the following magic words: "As long as you keep her [your Swan] on her medication, she'll be fine."

Of course, if your Swan is marrying a really Big Fish or, better yet, a Whale, the wise Mountaineer should not, under any circumstances, encourage the ex-boyfriend (or girlfriend) to make an incendiary toast. In fact, you should do any and everything to make sure the Swan actually goes through with the marriage. Yes, in the short run your Swan will desert you for the Big Fish or Whale spouse. But when the inevitable divorce happens, you will be there to make sure your Swan's alimony settlement includes unlimited use of her ex's private plane, and your Swan will soon be jetting you off to even better parties.

Weddings

The fantasy of the bride in white conjures up such potent and positive voodoo, everyone at the wedding begins to see the world through rose-colored glasses. However, that only works to the social climbers' advantage if they steel themselves against contamination and do not fall victim to the spell of wedding fever themselves and waste time and attention charming guests who have even less to offer than themselves. Linger with the maiden aunts from Wisconsin who can only invite you to the opening of a can of creamed corn no longer than it takes to make you seem like a caring person to people who can help you. Stay focused on what you came to the wedding to do—climb.

While weddings offer a romantic respite from the cynicism of modern life to the civilian, to the climber they provide a hearts-and-flowers version of von Clausewitz's fog of war, a veritable cloudbank of romantic delusion that makes even the clumsiest climber seem like an upwardly mobile Fred Astaire.

As to how to negotiate the wedding, know that most large weddings are basically dinner dances with pagan overtones and small weddings are generally for people who've been married before and lost most of their friends to the more successful ex, or those whose parents are too cheap to spring for a blowout. Basic cocktail party and dinner dance rules apply. In the postreligious service predinner cocktail stage of the party, it's best to stay moving. You are a shark, not a bottom-feeder. Meet, greet, and ascertain the worth of the guests as quickly as possible. Pretend to go to the bar, but do not drink at the bar. And even if you have the good fortune to be attending a no-expense-spared nuptial, do not keep hitting on the waitress carrying the tray of glasses brimming with champagne simply because it is free.

It's important to remember who brides and grooms and their parents invite to the wedding. Yes, there are the embarrassing family relations and lame friends from college they have to include. But invariably, brides and their family, when drawing up the guest list for a wedding, make a point of sending invitations to their most accomplished, successful, well-off, generous, and most-connected friends and relations, in part to get maximum return for their investment vis-à-vis expensive wedding presents.

And because even the most average groom's parents will compete with the bride's parents to show off just how many rich, successful, famous people they know, weddings are tantamount to Big Fish conventions. Not just local Big Fish, but Big Fish from other cities, different parts of the country, other nations. Most important of all, because Big Fish have seen so much ugliness while climbing their way to the top, they are particularly prone to fall under the spell of wedding witchcraft and open themselves up to becoming new best friends with you.

The simple fact that the bride's guests don't often know the groom's guests gives the climber still another advantage; whereas, at a normal party, it would be gauche to point and ask, "What's the name of that nice old man who drove up in the Rolls-Royce convertible?" or inquire bluntly, "Are those diamonds that woman's wearing real?," at a wedding, it's acceptable. There's no need to go to the bathroom and google one's fellow wedding guests because families from both sides of the aisle will be eager to brag about the net worth, claim to fame, or ostentatious lifestyle of every Big Fish they've managed to corral into the tent. Though bloodied bedsheets are no longer displayed to the guests after the wedding night, the great news for climbers is that weddings are still all about showing off. And when people are showing off how rich, famous, and successful they are, it's easy for even the visually impaired climber to see who merits chatting up.

Small weddings—intimate affairs of fewer than fifty guests—offer the added advantage of giving you the time and opportunity to meet all the Big Fish, even if you're stuck seated between the two maiden aunts with the creamed corn. At a large wedding, those with more than 150 guests, it will be harder for you to stand out but much easier to switch place cards to a seat next to a Big Fish, Whale, Swan, Turtle, etc.

In our experience, the ideal wedding from a social climber's point of view is a midsize destination wedding, where a hundred or so guests are flown gratis to a five-star hotel with a pink sand beach. However, when one is a guest at a wedding held in a country where one does not speak the language, it is wise to keep a list of vital party information on your person at all times. Ms. Johnson learned this painful lesson when attending a gala nuptial of close personal friends on the island of Ibiza. The after-party for the rehearsal dinner took place in the VIP section of the island's nightclub of choice, Pasha, on a night DJ'ed by none other than David Guetta. All was fabu until Ms. Johnson made the mistake of leaving the VIP section to go to the ladies' room. On her return she was shocked and embarrassed to discover that the bouncer would not let her reenter due to the fact that she had forgotten the name of her host, the bridegroom. As Ms. Johnson learned the hard way, it is both bad manners and inconvenient to forget your host's name.

Perks and free plane fare alone don't make the difference between the great wedding and the merely good wedding. It's the number of new best friends you make. To do that, one has to stand out without being left out, which is another way of saying you need to stand out without others thinking you are trying to show off. And the best way to do that is to offer a toast to the newlyweds. Make it seem extemporaneous, but in fact you should have been polishing it in front of the mirror in the weeks leading up to the wedding. Do not be ashamed if you lack the writing skills to come up with a great toast on your own, i.e., either plagiarize or get an ex-boyfriend or -girlfriend to help you write it, with the veiled promise you will bring them to the wedding with you, which of course you won't.

As at the engagement party, resist the temptation to compose a toast that makes you seem clever at the bride and groom's expense, or that makes reference to old boyfriends or girlfriends or the indiscretions that occurred at the bachelorette/bachelor party.

A word to the wise: The same feel-good feeling that makes weddings such an easy place to social climb also makes them treacherously dizzying for even the most experienced Mountaineer.

EMPOWERING THOUGHT #24

Social climbers are cynics, and cynics are disappointed romantics, i.e., even the most hardhearted Mountaineer will be tempted to get caught up in the infectious Last Night on the Planet to Mate vibe that permeates wedding parties. Do not pass up an opportunity to make a friendship that can advance you in order to exchange bodily fluids with a total stranger . . . no matter how long it has been since you have had sex.

Those social climbers invited to take part in the rehearsal dinner are particularly vulnerable to the sexual energy that is in the air. Mountaineers enlisted as bridesmaids and groomsmen are apt to find themselves thinking about the wrong kind of prize.

If you are unable to resist the urge to spawn at a wedding and take off your dress or trousers in a sand trap on the golf course or in the parking area, make a point of remembering where you left them. If you cannot remember, ask a valet parker for help finding them. Asking the bride's mother to help you find clothes misplaced in the heat of a quickie is one of the few forms of twenty-first-century wedding behavior that is universally deemed unacceptable.

11

WHAT AM I SAYING YES TO?
DATING, LOVE, AND MARRIAGE

There is no question that today's more casual approach to dating, courtship, and social intercourse of a sexual nature has provided climbing opportunities to upwardly mobile members of both sexes and all sexual orientations that were not available to previous generations of climbers.

Loosely arranged dinners and bar hangs involving groups of young climbers in their twenties, what we call Posse Dating, provides multiple climbing options. Unfettered by the commitments and obligations involved in having to go through the boring rigmarole of actually asking someone out for an old-fashioned date and having to spend the whole evening sitting next to that person, one is free to ditch the group with little or no guilt and climb solo when one runs into a superior class of person or group to get sloppy drunk with.

Better still, the Posse Date allows an individual who left the group to pursue a Big Fish but fails to land him or her the chance to rejoin the posse before the evening's over. Most important, if you return to the posse before last call, you will still have a shot at hooking up with one of the posse members, i.e., a friend with benefits. If you can't get a piece of the cake you really want to cut into, there's still cake to be had; or, as we say, skilled social climbers never miss an opportunity to have their cake and eat it, too.

Whether you are out there making the most of the no-strings group dating scene, or are an old-fashioned romantic type who dates just one person at a time in order to steal their best/most helpful friends more efficiently before trading up, nearly every Mountaineer eventually experiences a Come to Jesus moment. A moment when no matter how social climbing has improved your life, no matter how many Big Fish, Whales, Swans, Turtles, friends with benefits you have on speed dial, you sense something important is missing in your life. What sort of something? No, it's not a Ferrari or a set of identical twins who give backrubs and own a *schloss* in Gstaad. What you're lacking is a partner, a soul mate to climb with.

> For you this moment may come as an epiphany—a sudden realization that the fact you will never be able to love another person as much as yourself does not mean you are shallow, it means you are finally ready to have a mature relationship.

Others come to this crossroads because they hear the tick-tock of their biological clock. The sight of nannies pushing in-vitro twins who belong to a couple with matching Porsches often inspires climbers to wish they had a life partner they could have children with and share the joy of teaching the little ones how to climb. Some come to this Rubicon because their climb has leveled off. Having hit a plateau or, worse, having found themselves slipping backward, they muster up the humility to cling to someone else who is backsliding. Only as a couple pooling their address books and invites can they make it to the next level of the game.

EMPOWERING THOUGHT #25

True love for the Mountaineer comes when you meet someone you actually like, with whom you have hot sex as often as you eat, and who has so much more of everything than you do that you feel as if you've slept your way to the top, even if you didn't sleep your way to the top. Which, if you think about it, is how love should always feel.

Admittedly, it's hard to know whether you are thinking about getting serious because all of your friends with benefits have gotten married or stopped having casual sex with you, or because it actually *is* time for you to get serious about getting serious.

To find out if you are ready to give up climbing solo, answer the following questions:

1. Would you be more popular with the people you want to be popular with if you didn't sleep around? Yes / No

2. Is there an extra man or woman in your social set who is smarter, more accomplished, more attractive than you are who is suddenly scooping up all the invites you used to get? Yes / No

3. Would you have more money for social climbing if you had someone to split household expenses with and provide you with a marital deduction for your income tax? Yes / No

4. Is there a club you'd like to join but can't, because it doesn't accept unmarried women or men, or you lack the social credentials to get in on your own? Yes / No

5. Have you recently lost your job, and/or are you about to be indicted for a felony? Yes / No

6. Do you dream of being married to someone who owns a yacht and want to climb onboard while you still look good in a bathing suit? Yes / No

7. Will you inherit more money if you get married and/or have children? Yes / No

8. Do you know a Big Fish or Whale who's recently been ditched you think might be so heartbroken that he or she would say yes to marrying someone like yourself? Yes / No

9. Are you losing your hair or having trouble maintaining your youthful figure, or do you have a worsening medical condition that requires treatment not covered by your insurance carrier? Yes / No

If you have answered yes to any of the above, then it's time to get serious.

> To begin with, if you're serious about getting serious, you must put your hand on *The Social Climber's Bible* and swear from this moment on you will give up Posse Dating.

Yes, it will be hard to get used to actually calling someone up on a phone and asking that person out, but trust us: This modus operandi is so quaint, whoever you ask out will mistake your directness for self-confidence rather than desperation. Equally important: no more bottom-feeding, even when you're lonely.

From this moment on, you must also swear you will only date Keepers.

If you have already dated your way up the food chain and are involved with a Big Fish who laughed the last time you brought up the subject of marriage, or is already married but claims he/she can't divorce because of the negative psychological effect on their children or because their spouse has threatened to commit suicide, do not believe them. These are lame excuses. Know that if they really valued you or your sexual favors they would be worried about you threatening to kill yourself. Regardless, it's time to move on . . . but on your terms, not theirs.

To put yourself in the best position to find a Keeper, you will have to get rid of the Big Fish in a way that generates sympathy for you among your Big Fish's friends, so you can keep fishing in his/her pond—i.e., you have to make it seem that Mr. or Ms. Big Fish has dumped you rather than vice versa. How do you do that? Dose him/her with a hit of X, invite over your trampiest friend, and leave the house. Come back two hours later and walk in on them *en flagrante*. Get upset, but make it clear that you forgive both of them and still want to be friends, i.e., still go to their parties, sleep with their friends, but not sleep with them because you can't bear to have your heart broken again.

Fortunately, we live in a time in which interracial and interfaith unions are accepted. But as much as the world has changed, a mixed marriage between a social climber and a non–social climber poses special challenges and puts often insurmountable strains on the relationship from day one.

Will your prospective spouse convert to your faith? Will they ever care enough about you to go out and make the kind of friends that will help you get to the top of the mountain? Or will they insist on including their white trash friends and family in your social life? Can a nonpracticing social climber teach your child the commandments contained in *The Social Climbers Bible*?

Since 99 percent of avowed non-social climbers are simply closeted climbers or "networkers" hiding behind semantics, many of the differences between practicing and non-practicing social climbers can be worked out through the help of therapy and/or withholding sex.

If your spouse is to be your fellow Mountaineer for better or for worse, it's important that you familiarize each other with any and all confabulations you have told to each other or to anyone else in the process of making yourself seem more desirable. Total transparency is essential. If your significant other reveals that the year she spent teaching prison inmates learn to read was the same year she did time for check kiting, don't hold it against her. Instead, ask her to get your back by swearing she visited you and David Foster Wallace at the psychiatric hospital you never went to or had tea with that nonexistent grandmother you've told everyone took you on safari when you were a child. In order to help each other, you have to be honest about just how much help you really need.

Of course the social climber should not complicate a serious relationship by being needlessly honest.

To increase your chances of finding a Keeper who loves social climbing as much as you do, it's important to keep dating others even after you've succeeded in getting serious about someone. Why? Because the odds are he or she is doing it on the sly, too. Keep your options open and make a point of never referring to these dates as "dates." Simply say you're going to dinner without your Keeper boyfriend/girlfriend because a friend of yours has a problem he's not comfortable discussing with anyone but you. By being discreet yet open, you can still have the opportunity to hook up with someone who's even more of a Keeper than the Keeper you found, while you're officially getting serious. We call this Hedge Bet Dating.

In our opinion, it's okay to have Hedge Bet Sex once a week up until the wedding invitations go out. After that, limit your extracurricular fishing expeditions to lunch dates.

What to Do When the Big Moment Finally Arrives

The biggest moment for the social climber who's gotten serious comes not when one half of the couple drops to one knee and the carat count of the engagement stone is revealed. Nor is it that really big moment when you actually say "I do" and the bond between you and your partner is legally binding. No, the really, really big moment we're talking about comes when a climber's future spouse first brings up the subject of a prenuptial agreement.

> If you are the one who is asking your future partner to sign a prenup, you are doing so because your net worth is significantly greater than your fiancé's. If he balks, takes offense, and accuses you of being unromantic to even broach the subject of a prenuptial agreement, the question you should be asking yourself at this point is not whether he is a gold digger, but rather, why are you about to marry someone who has so much less to offer than you do?

If you have the "money" and your spouse-to-be has the "class," i.e., comes from a more socially prominent and well-connected family that has fallen on hard times but still has social clout, entrée you do not possess, be realistic! Know that when you marry into a grand family that's on the financial skids, the siblings and/or parents will start hitting you up to borrow money before you've left on your honeymoon. Also know that they will think you cheap if you request an IOU and won't ever pay you back even if you get one.

> If you are subhandsome/less-than-gorgeous rich, and the penniless spouse-to-be who calls you unromantic for asking her or him to sign a prenup is drop-dead gorgeous, know that you're not only dealing with a gold digger, but also dealing with a gold digger who thinks you're stupid and subattractive.

Stop being so superficial and look in the mirror. Find yourself a life partner who's as less than gorgeous as yourself but has more of the important things in life than you do, i.e., someone who's in a position to ask you to sign a prenup.

More than likely, if you're reading *The Social Climber's Bible* when you're getting serious about someone, you will be the one asked to sign the prenup. When the subject first comes up, do not get upset, cry, or accuse your spouse-to-be of thinking you're a gold digger.

Prepare for the inevitable prenup conversation moment by familiarizing yourself with your husband- or wife-to-be's finances. While he is off shopping for the engagement ring, and/ or she is returning the embarrassingly small zircon you gave her, photocopy any and all legal/financial papers you can find in their desk and ransack the hard drive of their computer. Pay particular attention to deeds, stock transfers, trust instruments, off-shore accounts held in the name of shell companies, etc. Make sure you have a clear understanding of what your future spouse is worth. There's nothing sneaky about your making sure they have not been sneaky.

If you have prepared yourself in this way, when the subject of the prenup is first mentioned, it'll be easier for you to smile and say, "All I want is *you*. If a prenup makes you feel better, I'm happy to sign anything you want."

Having made them feel guilty, have sex with them. Afterward, say they are the "most giving lover in the world." Which should make them feel doubly guilty. If your fiancé has not presented you with the prenup two weeks before the wedding, do not be lulled into thinking they have decided you're such a superior human being, a prenup is unnecessary. Know that your fiancé is merely planning on having a notary at the rehearsal dinner to get you to sign without showing it to your lawyer.

If they still have not produced a legal document two weeks before the wedding, "flip it" and tell them sweetly, "No prenup, no wedding." When they finally do produce the prenuptial agreement, you will of course be curious to see, in the event of divorce, just how much in terms of dollars and cents your future spouse thinks each year of sex with you is worth. Resist the temptation to look at the numbers. Instead, take your spouse-to-be's face in your hands, and tell them you have never been happier in your life. That one day the two of you will be celebrating your fiftieth anniversary and that you don't even need to read the prenup, because the two of you are too in love to ever think about divorce, much less get one. This will make them feel even more guilty, but not so guilty they don't quickly flip to the last page and whip out a pen for you to sign on the dotted line.

We suggest that the social climber who's marrying into the one percent turn the big moment into *your* big moment. Kiss them passionately as you take pen in hand and suggest in your sexiest voice that the two of you put off signing just long enough to have a quickie. Do not be surprised when your future spouse suggests that he/she will screw you after you sign. Now look at the dotted line and sigh, "I really want to put this behind us, but my mother made me promise I'd never sign any legal papers until I showed them to a lawyer." By inserting your mother into the equation you ensure that your spouse will accuse her, not you, of mistrusting him/her.

If your future wife/husband then proceeds to give you the name of a great lawyer, particularly if he/she is a member of a multigenerational-wealth family, you have now been officially alerted that you are about to be screwed. If you cannot afford to retain a lawyer equal to or better than your future spouse's legal counsel, sign a promissory note guaranteeing an equally prestigious firm a percentage of any future divorce settlement.

If the terms of the prenup are insulting, do not take it personally. Let your lawyer take it personally. Generally speaking, a prenup guarantees the spouse coming into the marriage with fewer assets a fixed amount of money for each year of predivorce bliss. If you are marrying a Big Fish, you can expect he or she will cover your basic postdivorce expenses for somewhere between two and five years. However, if you've been caught cheating on your spouse, basic expenses will be very basic.

If you're lucky enough to be marrying a Whale, three to five years of marriage puts you on the payroll for life. Or until they get one of their Whale friends to marry you to remove you from the payroll. The big payoff in Whale prenups comes if the marriage produces children. The poorer parent can expect to be guaranteed a home and lifestyle equal to that of the richer parent so that the offspring won't be too embarrassed to spend court-appointed days and nights with poor dad/poor mom.

All that being said, we believe that the important thing for all Mountaineers who are marrying into money to realize is, your wedding day should be a special moment unsullied by thoughts of divorce and cash settlements. If your prenuptial negotiations threaten to delay the wedding, and/or your future husband/wife insists on playing hardball regarding the terms of the prenup, take the high road, sign, and enjoy the party.

Why give up? Because you're not giving up, you're just making it seem as if you're a less greedy person than your well-heeled spouse. Even the best prenuptial agreement, like the best marriage, is an act of good faith. Know that any and all prenuptial agreements can be renegotiated in your favor at a future point in time—if you make the marriage hellish enough.

The Other Big Moment—Your Wedding

Whether you're a Mountaineer who's marrying up or one who's tying the knot because you think you'll get to the top faster by working as a team, your wedding is an opportunity to climb.

EMPOWERING THOUGHT #26

Remember: your wedding is a special day for you and your most special friends, i.e., those who have more social clout, business connections, celebrity, money, etc., than you do. Ideally, the climber getting married should be the least successful person at the wedding!

A wedding is not an opportunity for you to show off how well you're doing to the friends and family you left behind when you started social climbing. You can convey this information in a Christmas card that features an envy-inspiring photo of you and your spouse frolicking exotically on your honeymoon. If for sentimental reasons you feel obliged to send invitations to embarrassing siblings, parents, etc., hold the wedding in a foreign country so that you can be sure they won't be able to afford to attend.

WARNING

Those who have signed a prenup and whose more financially well-endowed fiancé lobbies for a dream wedding in an exotic locale, beware! For example, having a Buddhist priest perform the ceremony in a Balinese temple is definitely romantic. Unfortunately, when you return to the United States, unless you have a legally binding certificate to go with that Buddhist priest's blessing, you will not be legally wed and the prenup you worked so hard to negotiate will be of no value. It is the poorer spouse's responsibility to check with legal authorities to make sure that when your slippery Big Fish says "I do," he or she will still be on the hook when you get back to the United States.

Likewise, for those who have signed a prenup, if something untoward occurs in the course of the prewedding festivities, say your wife-to-be has sex with one of the male strippers at her bachelorette party, or your husband-to-be insists on inviting all his ex-wives, do not call off the wedding, especially if someone else is paying for it. Make as many new friends as possible and get even by making out with the cute groomsman or hot bridesmaid and fantasize about them when you have sex with your spouse on the honeymoon.

The Honeymoon

Going away to a deserted beach or on a deluxe safari for two in the wild sounds romantic, but in fact the majority of upwardly mobile newlyweds will find that being holed up with the person they've just agreed to spend the rest of their life with as isolating as entering the witness protection program. You cannot social climb on a deserted beach or in the middle of the jungle.

Instead, we recommend taking a honeymoon in a cushy resort where you'll be able to hobnob with the game changers who in all likelihood were not at your wedding, i.e., Big Fish and Whales.

EMPOWERING THOUGHT #27

Because being newlyweds makes you a "cute couple" (even if you are not cute) and Big Fish and Whales are sentimental, especially when bombed and on holiday, it will be easy for you to make friends with somebodies who wouldn't think you were sweet and charming if they were back home and sober.

When the Honeymoon Is Over

You are now married. After you finish writing the thank-you notes for all the gifts you have received, certain grim realities may soon become apparent to one or both of you. The little things your spouse does that you used to think were endearing will seem less endearing—teeth grinding, snoring, urinating on the toilet seat, cleaning ears with Q-tips at the breakfast table, etc. You will become frustrated with each other due in part to the fact that Hedge Bet Dating is no longer a socially acceptable way to blow off steam. And you will soon realize that in most marriages one partner becomes the gardener and the other the garden, which is a drag, especially if you are the gardener. If only one of you is spending all your time on your hands and knees, know that your marriage is in trouble . . . but it doesn't have to be that way.

A marriage between two social climbers who share the same goals and aspirations has a greater chance of success, because those married Mountaineers will recognize that tending to each other's petty needs is not going to make their hopes and dreams come true. The good news is, neither spouse has to be a gardener if the two of you can gain access to gardens more lavish and bountiful than those you could ever grow in your own backyard.

Whereas in most marriages, after a year or two of cohabitation familiarity begins to breed contempt, married social climbers spend so much time out and about working hard to make new friends who can help them that when they get home they are too tired to bicker. Similarly, social climbing spouses are less prone to fall victim to the sexual boredom that inevitably plagues many marriages. When you are working together to seduce a Big Fish, or better yet a Whale, you will get the same seductive thrill and self-affirmation that less sophisticated couples can only find in extramarital affairs. Whether one or both of you has to sleep with the Whale you're trying to befriend is up to you. The point is: It's a team effort, not a selfish act.

Upward mobility gives a marriage purpose. You both know the direction you are heading: *to the top!* You go to a cocktail party with a joint game plan, and the synergy of your social climbing skills helps you climb faster than either one of you could alone. That's what you love most about your partner and what makes marriage both fun and profitable.

Sadly, God did not create all social climbers equal. If you see your husband spending more time on the practice range than networking out on the greens, you have reason to worry that one member of the team has taken his eye off the ball. When a spouse turns down an invitation to a dinner party given by a Big Fish because she "doesn't feel like getting dressed up" and "just wants to veg," know that there are cracks in the foundation of your marriage. If you feel your partner is not doing their fair share of the climbing, if he or she still wants to stay home and veg instead of meeting new and exciting people who can help *you*, know that in the long run you will be doing both of you a favor if you go back to climbing solo.

Yes, you will be heartbroken, but divorce is the best thing that happens to most marriages. Any psychologist will tell you, it's never one person's fault, even if you're the one who got caught having sex with your spouse's brother/sister. We know you wouldn't have done it if your spouse had been out there climbing with you instead of vegging at home. Know that your marriage ended for the same reason that over half the marriages in the world end in divorce—one member of the team didn't have enough self-love to give a hundred percent. And if you are married to someone who doesn't love him- or herself enough to know that they deserve the best, you cannot expect that person to love you or what you love, i.e., social climbing.

You, as a shrewd social climber, should always stay "friends" with your exes no matter how much you hate them, no matter what they have called you, or even if they have dumped you. Remember the Mountaineer is always in control of his or her emotions. If you have not yet attained that level of self-control, "fake it and flip it," i.e., tell the bastard/bitch, "I will always love you and be there for you." If you have trouble making those words come out of your mouth without gagging, practice saying them in front of the mirror.

EMPOWERING THOUGHT #28

Always speak fondly of your ex-spouse in public, even if he or she is trashing you about town and emailing compromising naked photos of you to your boss/business associates/children. Why? Because you are a Mountaineer, and by taking the high road and letting your ex do the bad-mouthing for both of you, everyone will assume that they were "the problem."

No matter how acrimonious the divorce, say enough nice things about your ex and your ex will begin to believe that they were the problem even if in fact they weren't. Eventually, the ex will stop blaming you and start inviting you to their parties, especially if you have traded up and are now married to a Big Fish/Whale your ex wants to become friends with.

12

A VIRTUAL NEW YOU

It's not what you are, but what they think
you are that is important.

—Joseph Kennedy

t's time to get back on Facebook and use social media to introduce people to the person you want them to think you are. Not just the new you, the virtual new you! By now, if you've been doing your homework and following our suggestions, you should have at the very least become new best friends with two Big Fish and acquired a Swan and/or Turtle, all of whom are bringing you to parties, dinners, openings, charity events, weddings, and at least one star-studded funeral. If the above doesn't sound like your life, you should consider doing what our friends from Landmark Forum call revisiting your "story" and take responsibility for the excuses that are holding you back from realizing your true potential. In other words, get over yourself, climb out of the pity pot, and try harder.

Returning to social media will give your social cred a bump by legitimizing the new and improved person you've become since you started reading this book and owned up to your dreams.

Your new Facebook page is the first step you will be taking to turn your persona into a brand as deluxe as an Hermès bag, as synonymous with good taste as Cristal champagne, and as popular as Google. Remember, though people love Google for its integrity, as expressed in its unofficial motto, "Don't be evil," you, unfortunately, are not a corporation worth hundreds of billions of dollars, i.e., your personal motto should be "Admire most those who help you most."

Think of your new Facebook page as the twenty-first-century equivalent of the nineteenth-century calling card. Two hundred years ago, when a gentleman came to town and wanted to announce his arrival, he had his servant drop a card at the home of the person he wanted to suck up to. If he was especially eager to make that person's acquaintance, he would fold a corner of the card to indicate he had dropped it off in person.

Think of the message you want to send as your cyber calling card. The details, quality, and good taste of your new Facebook page will determine what we call your friendability.

> Your new Facebook page should not make you seem as if you're boasting, but it should convey the distinct illusion that you know many more fabulous and famous people than you actually do, and that those reading your page should friend you now while you're still accepting friends. This is your chance to offer those who have reserved judgment about you a virtual look at who you really are—virtually.

Even though you removed your Facebook page back in Chapter 4, those humiliating photos of you could still come back to haunt you. If, for instance, your old page revealed that you like former New York Jets quarterback Mark Sanchez, Dr. Phil, and Snuggies, you now need to distance yourself from the loser you once were and the friends who tagged you in photos that make you look as large and undesirable as a secondhand sofa left on the side of the road. To avoid the possibility of your past coming back to bite you in your cyber-ass, now is the right time for you to change the name of your brand. If you were a Barney, you might want to become a Bernard. Wouldn't you rather be Françoise than Francie? Or, if you're feeling bold, give yourself a new surname as well. More than one of the reigning single socialites currently cashing in on their aristocratic lineage in New York wasn't born with the last name she is currently using to sell herself. We would be glad to give you her initials, except we fear we would be sued. Happy with your name as it is? Add a new middle initial, and if photos of the old you do resurface, you can explain that your old self is a distant relation you haven't seen in years.

By now, if you have been following our advice, you should have a collection of selfies, photos of yourself with important people you have never even met, as well as pictures of you with the two Big Fish and Turtle who have become your NBFs. Post one of each on your page and if, for example, the three strangers you've taken selfies of or had yourself photographed standing next to are, say, Salman Rushdie, Ryan Seacrest, and Fran Lebowitz, when your Turtle and Big Fish friends check out your page, they'll not only see themselves with you but they'll also see you hanging with Salman, Ryan, and Fran; chances are they would like to meet your celebrity pals and will send you a Friend Request.

A social climber should never send a Friend Request even if he or she does get lucky enough to actually meet Salman, Ryan, or Fran. And remember, even if a somebody you have been desperate to connect with for months tries to Friend you, always wait forty-eight hours before accepting the invitation.

> A social climber should never appear desperate and/or needy, especially if he or she is.

Naturally, your new friends will wonder why you have deemed them unworthy of a real-life introduction to Salman, Ryan, and Fran. The best answer to this question is, "They're very private people." Which, of course, will also make them wonder who else you know whom you haven't yet introduced them to. If you're pals with Fran, does that mean you're hanging with *Vanity Fair* editor Graydon Carter? And if you're buds with Ryan Seacrest, maybe if they were a little nicer to you, you'd invite them along when you hang out with *The Voice* judges Adam Levine and Blake Shelton?

EMPOWERING THOUGHT #29

The ideal Facebook page should make you seem fabulous enough to be worth getting to know better, but not so fabulous as to be intimidating or to inspire resentment. You also don't want it to appear that you are only interested in friending Big Fish and somebodies, which is true, but not something you should advertise.

Of course, this is a fine line to tread. One of the best ways to seem less superficial than you are is to post excerpts and/or editorials from foreign newspapers—*The Guardian*, *Figaro*, *Die Zeit*. You don't have to be able to read them, just having their links on your Facebook page will make you seem more intelligent to others, and to yourself.

Facebook is your chance to add veracity to any elements of your backstory that you have exaggerated or invented in the course of making friends with Swans, Turtles, and Big Fish. If, for example, you told people your grandmother took you on safari in Africa, leaf through old copies of *National Geographic* for an old photo of a woman and a child with an elephant. Post it, with the caption "Me and Granny on the Serengeti Plain, 1983." If you get comments that you don't look like the child, tell them you've changed. That much is true.

It's important that you do not try to supply pictorial evidence to support all the whoppers you've told and dead famous friends you have name-dropped since you started climbing all at once. Spread them out over the coming months as you update your status. Be subtle. If, for instance, you told people you biked across Tasmania with Heath Ledger, post a snapshot of two beat-up mountain bikes lying forlornly in the grass and simply write, "Heath's bike." Let them ask you, "Heath who?" Sometimes less is more when social climbing on the Internet.

Your Facebook page is you. Make it worthy enough, and someone might invite you to join the thinking snob's version of Facebook, ASMALLWORLD, an invitation-only network capped at a mere 250,000, which promises to make you "feel at home anywhere." Tellingly, it was conceived by Count Erik Wachtmeister, the son of the former Swedish ambassador to the United States, while he was wild-boar hunting in Germany, and is designed to put members in touch with "a community of global nomads who hang out together," i.e., people who inherited enough money so they don't have to have a real job. There's no question that it is truly a small world; when we first met Count Erik in New York in the eighties, he was a hard-partying Big Fish whose popularity with fashion models earned him a nickname that our lawyers have advised us not to repeat. The point is, if Erik can rebrand himself, so can you.

In principle, we are against any virtual venue for self-promotion that doesn't give the fledgling climber a shot at the top. However, if you do con someone into inviting you to join ASmallWorld or any other überexclusive site, your membership will only add to the veracity of your embellished exotic backstory and enable you to meet even more advanced social climbers than yourself. Remember, there's nothing like watching a roomful of great Mountaineers in action to teach even the most experienced climber new tricks.

Tweeting Your Way into the Winner's Circle

Tweeting has revolutionized and democratized social climbing. Next to your charm, your iPhone, Droid, Samsung Galaxy, or whatever is the single most essential tool a climber possesses.

Say you're at a party for Prada's new strapless heel, or Mark Wahlberg's latest movie. If you write in 140 characters or less why the shoe or the film is fantastic and attach a picture of yourself having a fabulous time at the launch, you're not bragging to the ether that you got invited to an exclusive event, you're sharing your life and turning your friends, both real and virtual, on to a product you think is wonderful.

More important, subliminally you're also saying your brand—i.e., you—is a product on par with Prada or Mark Wahlberg. If Ashton Kutcher can get over fourteen million people to follow his tweets, why can't you?

If your answer to that question is a self-pitying, "Because he's Ashton Kutcher and I'm not," you need an attitude adjustment.

Stop making excuses for yourself and get creative. All you need is your iPhone, a little ingenuity, and some imagination. Say there's a gala for a Mark Wahlberg movie premiere sponsored by Louis Vuitton/Chopard/Hewlett-Packard. If you've been doing your homework, you will observe that the press and paparazzi photos of the somebodies, celebrities, and Big Fish at last year's gala were taken against a blue backdrop plastered with corporate logos. While people who have been invited to the gala are getting dressed to go to the gala, you get dressed up, too. Put on your tux or slinkiest cocktail dress. Now take a photo of yourself and superpose it against the Louis Vuitton backdrop you've lifted from last year's photos of the event. Once you get one that makes you look good and seems believable, wait until the party you aren't at and haven't been invited to is just getting good, then tweet that you "# ♥ LV" or Mark Wahlberg's movie is a "must-see" and attach the photo you've created of yourself on the red carpet.

Now, don't answer your phone until the next morning, leading all your friends, virtual and real, to believe that while you're sitting at home alone all dressed up with no place to go, you were in fact too busy having an awesome time at the party to answer.

The next morning, after you read about the after-party on "Page Six," turn your phone back on and tweet that you're too hungover to tweet the details of what a fabulous time you had last night with all the celebrities you now know attended the after-after-party at the Standard hotel's Boom Boom Room.

Remember: When tweeting yourself into fantastic events that you weren't invited to, always gush positive and instruct the ever-growing number of people who are following your virtual but truly fantastic life to immediately go out and buy the shoes, see the movie, and purchase whatever products the sponsors are selling.

Do this often enough, and convincingly enough, and eventually those sponsors, and their PR flacks, will start actually sending you invitations to the kinds of events you need to go to to make your real life live up to the virtual life that has spawned the person you now have genuinely become.

Instagramming from a posh, desirable, elite location is your way of substantiating the authenticity of the lifestyle you want people to think you're living but cannot yet afford to live.

Say you'd like to be perceived as the kind of person who lunches at Nobu but lack the wherewithal to afford even a single slice of their signature sushi. All you have to do to make people think you're having lunch at Nobu is to stop by at lunchtime, tell the maître d' you're meeting friends but don't know the name the reservation was made under, and sit at the bar. Take an artful snap of a nearby plate of Black Cod with Miso, tweet how delicious it looks and how hungry you are and that you're lunching at Nobu.

Do this often enough, and you not only have a shot at becoming the kind of person who can afford to have lunch at Nobu, you'll also lose those pounds you put on while sitting around your house eating chips and onion dip while pretending to go to premieres you weren't invited to.

Pinterest a pic of a 1964 Ferrari Dino you see parked on the street and post, "Love this Ferrari 'cause it reminds me of the one Mom drove me to school in." With the Internet, it's all up to you, and people will think you're almost as cool as your mom.

Worried about getting caught? Or leaving a cyber-trail that will be used against you when all the social climbing tricks we've taught you are about to pay off and you're on the verge of getting engaged to Prince Harry, or being made partner at Goldman Sachs? Post your confabulations with Snapchat and the self-promoting lies you post about yourself will be permanently erased from cyberspace after ten seconds.

Undoubtedly there will be newer and more effective cyber tools to help you climb by the time you're reading this book.

> The important thing is to use any and all means at your disposal to make it seem that you're having more fun in your virtual life than you do in your real life.

If you have a modicum of imagination, Facebook, Twitter, Instagram, Pinterest, Snapchat, and whatever is the next social networking tool to come down the pike, when worked in conjunction, will not only allow you to redefine yourself but are a venue to offer proof that you have the same taste and lifestyle as the people you want to get to know, even if you have not acquired the kind of friends who can help you live out those aspirations.

Put up enough flags in cyberspace and someone will salute you.

13

NETWORKING: HOW TO WIN FRIENDS, INFLUENCE PEOPLE, AND USE THEM TO TURN A PROFIT

In today's postrecession economic hard times, social climbing for financial gain, aka networking, is a no-brainer. The origin of the expression says everything about the world's hypocritical attitude regarding the social climber. One would expect an expression like "networking" to have come out of a bastion of capitalism like the Harvard Business School. But in fact the word was first concocted by radical sixties counterculture icon and social activist Jerry Rubin. Mr. Rubin coined this expression after his politics took a sudden right turn. Realizing that "wealth creation is the real revolution," Rubin began to throw parties where the people he used to call "capitalist pigs" would be charged admission for the opportunity to meet other "capitalist pigs," i.e., networking. Clearly, Mr. Rubin was too embarrassed to call his scheme what it actually was: Mountaineering for money.

Jerry Rubin's reluctance to tell it like it is speaks to a basic attitudinal and philosophical divide that separates the two basic schools of entrepreneurial Mountaineering (networking)—those who maintain that they only social climb to make money versus those who insist they make money in order to social climb.

EMPOWERING THOUGHT #30

Those who claim they are only social climbing to make money are implying that there is something crass about social climbing, whereas those who maintain that they make money in order to social climb suggest there is something crass about money. In our opinion, both subspecies of networker are missing the point—social climbing should be both fun and profitable.

If you are one of those Mountaineers who feel the need to rationalize their climb with profit, you are still operating under the pernicious and hypocritically false value system that has demonized social climbing. To those readers we say: Stop hating yourself, come out of the closet, and take pride in what you are. Likewise, to those of you in the other camp who take false pride in boasting that you only make money so you can enjoy the pleasures of social climbing, we say, own up to your greed.

Strange but true, 99 percent of those same small-minded souls who will call you a brownnoser/asslicker/social climber for engineering an invitation that will allow you to enjoy the company of those more celebrated, famous, accomplished, or re-fined than yourself will turn on a moral dime and proceed to call you smart, clever, a go-getter for sucking up via tennis, golf, PTA meetings, etc., to get something as mundane as a raise.

EMPOWERING THOUGHT #31

The fact that monetary profit turns asslicking into networking says much about the voodoo of money. Following that twisted line of logic, the exchange of cash would make prostitution admirable and nonprofit sex, i.e., love, against the law. All networkers are social climbers but not all social climbers are networkers.

To us at *The Social Climber's Bible*, there seems to be a con-spiracy at work at the highest level of the entrepreneurial com-munity. Talk to any Big Fish in the financial world, and the first boastful excuse they'll make in defending their obscene salaries is that the world of finance, like America, is a "meritocracy." Which, by implication, is a good thing. The only trouble with that line of thought is that is not what the word "meritocracy" means.

Look it up. It's not a good thing. Especially not for social climbers. "Meritocracy" was a word coined to describe how the English class system in the mid-twentieth century was designed to keep the haves on top and the have-nots on the bottom.

Know this: Big Fish and Whales do not misuse the word "meritocracy" by accident. They do it diabolically and deliberately. They have redefined a pejorative as a positive to trick you with a carrot that isn't a carrot. Why? Because they want to be the only ones who know the system is rigged so that networkers who have networked into the right network win even if they lose money.

> Why should bankers be the only ones to fail upward? You can be as good at making bad investments as they can if you've social climbed your way into the "right" network.

If you have been following our advice in previous chapters, by now you have undoubtedly made at least one new best friend who is a Big Fish businessman/woman. Well done. Yes, it has been pretty fabulous just being able to hang out with somebody who's rich enough to spend more on wine at dinner than you make in a month. But honestly, aren't you getting a little bored simply being a great guest?

Given all the fun and polite conversation you've invested in your Big Fish friendship, isn't it about time you had something to show for it, other than that sunburn you got lying next to their swimming pool and all those blisters and bruises you endured playing endless games of tennis, golf, or touch football with your Big Fish and their children?

Do not be ashamed if you feel awkward or unsure about

how to turn a purely social friendship into a business relationship that's a can't-lose proposition for you. All social climbers feel that way before they turn their first Big Fish into a cash cow. Do not feel guilty about exploiting your first Big Fish—how do you think they got their start?

Unlike the denizens of Wall Street who boast about eating what they kill, you are merely taking your much-deserved pound of flesh. Also know that if you not only make money off your Big Fish by persuading him to invest in an idea or business opportunity but actually end up enabling him to turn a profit, he won't simply like you, he will love you!

So how does a social climber, aka a networker, who wants a Big Fish to invest in his/her gizmo or business scheme or who needs a job broach the subject of needing help?

To begin with, no matter how desperate your financial straits are or how long you have been unemployed, erase the thought that you are asking for help; you are offering the Big Fish an opportunity to help themselves by helping *you* get in a better position to make the Big Fish money . . . hopefully. You are doing your Big Fish a favor. And if you lose his money, he still owes you for trying.

For starters, say nothing about your business proposition or job request to anyone, most especially to the Big Fish you plan on approaching, who, for the purpose of this exercise, we will call Big Fish Bob. Stay off the subject of business entirely except to flatter Big Fish Bob for his business savvy. If, when you are in Big Fish Bob's presence, you witness someone else make a business proposition to Bob or if Bob asks your opinion of another's proposition, always subtly indicate how pathetic and foolish you find it that someone would stoop to exploiting a social friendship with a shrewd man like Bob for personal gain.

By now, you will know Big Fish Bob well enough to be aware of a second Big Fish that Bob either is in direct competition with or loathes due to the fact that he is either above or below Bob on the Big Fish food chain. We will call this one Big Fish Pete.

Without Big Fish Bob's knowledge, make the acquaintance of rival Big Fish Pete. How do you do that? By using your well-honed social climbing recon skills. Find out Pete's hobbies, people you know in common, etc. If you discover Pete has a passion for a rarefied pastime, say, for the purposes of this exercise, snail charting, read up enough to know that snail charting consists of putting a dot of colored nail polish on the shell of a snail and following it around for several days, mapping its routes though the garden. Arrange to bump into Pete and mention your fondness for live escargot and invite him to have lunch with you at the restaurant where you know Big Fish Bob has lunch.

Why will Big Fish Pete, whom you just met, say yes to lunch? Because you are a fellow snail charter, and because he knows you are friends with his enemy and competitor Big Fish Bob. Even if Pete doesn't like you, he will break bread with you in the hopes you will inadvertently say something that he can use against Big Fish Bob.

At your lunch with Pete, discuss neither your business proposition nor your friendship with Bob. Talk snails. When Big Fish Bob arrives at his favorite restaurant and sees you having lunch with Pete, pretend not to notice him. Make a show of laying a spreadsheet out on the table that shows the path of the imaginary snail you've been charting.

Guaranteed, within twenty-four hours of this lunch at which nothing but snails was discussed, you will get a call from Big Fish Bob inquiring why you were having lunch with someone as loathsome as Big Fish Pete. Reply that you asked his nemesis to lunch to discuss an investment opportunity or a job you want. Big Fish Bob, having seen you show Big Fish Pete papers, will assume they were business papers or your résumé, not a snail chart. At this point Bob is sure to say, "Why didn't you come to me with your business deal?" or, "Why didn't you ask me for help with a job?" At this point the cunning networker sinks the hook by confessing, "I didn't want to take advantage of our friendship."

Now that you have him on the line, play him carefully. Because Big Fish are competitive, Big Fish Bob will begin by telling you all the reasons you don't want to be in business with a knuckle-dragger like Big Fish Pete, or have a bottom-feeder like Pete get you a job.

Note: Big Fish often consider beating another Big Fish out of a deal a good deal, even if the deal is as lame as the one you will likely be offering them. Even if Bob does run with the bait and offer to help you then and there, hesitate. Tell Bob that you and Big Fish Pete shook on the deal and you are a man/woman of your word.

Big Fish Bob will then call Big Fish Pete and mention the fact that he saw you and Pete having lunch and ask what you were talking about. Know that when Pete tells Big Fish Bob the truth—that you were discussing snail charting—it is an absolute certainty that Big Fish Bob is going to think Pete is lying. And in Big Fish Bob's mind, if Pete is lying about what you were talking about at lunch, it means that your business proposition is a better proposition than it seemed when you relayed it to him or you have hidden skills that make you more qualified for the kind of job he assumes you asked Big Fish Pete to help you get. Either way, two or three days after Bob hangs up, he will call you back with an offer to team up with him. Say no twice before saying yes. You know you're screwing Big Fish Bob, but he doesn't.

Even after contracts are signed, the game is not over, not for a networker like you. Via the magic of networking, Big Fish Pete will hear about your new business deal with Bob or the new job Bob got you. Big Fish Pete, thinking he missed out on a chance to make money by talking snail charting with you, will now ask you out to lunch at a restaurant not frequented by Big Fish Bob to find out what other deals and ambitions you have simmering and offer to hook you up with bigger and better investors or a higher paying job.

Remember, you should always network within striking distance of at least two new potential bigger fish partners before jettisoning your first Big Fish business partner or getting fired. We say this not because we think you're going to be fired, or hope your deal goes south, but simply because whether your business fails isn't important, it's that *you* succeed that matters.

> ### Warning
> If you're a small fish, be on your guard when a Big Fish seems overly eager to be networked by you.

Mr. Wittenborn learned this in 1991 when he was introduced to the Big Fish of his dreams, a smart, savvy, no-nonsense film financier—new to New York—who happened to be Bill Gates's cousin. Yes, that Bill Gates. Most impressive of all, she wanted to give Mr. Wittenborn $5 million to make a movie. He and other aspiring filmmakers were thrilled to be approached by a woman who knew everyone in show business by their first name and had unlimited resources.

Not surprisingly, every networker in Manhattan homed in on her like heat-seeking missiles. Big Fish loaned her their limos and invited her to stay in the guest rooms of their penthouses. After a feverish month of being wined and dined, it turned out there was just one problem: This Big Fish of everyone's dreams was not Bill Gates's cousin.

The moral of this story? Networkers who promise to give people millions of dollars they don't have not only need psychiatric help, they also give honest, hardworking social climbers a bad name.

Genuine Big Fish who can lend support or, better yet, invest money in a social climber's dreams are called mentors. If you are that rare networker who actually possesses real business acumen, and if you succeed in using your mentor's money or connections to turn a profit for both you and the mentor, the Big Fish will want to remain your mentor.

Of course you will realize that if Big Fish A can enable you to make a hundred-thousand-dollar profit, even bigger Big Fish B could help you net a million. In short, your beloved mentor Big Fish will need to be upgraded about as often as the operating system on your Mac.

EMPOWERING THOUGHT #32

Do not feel guilty when it is time to leave your mentor behind, especially if you have made your soon-to-be-ex mentor money. Remind yourself that they are getting old, and if you linger, you will soon be helping your old mentor more than they are helping you—which is not what networking is all about.

Obviously, you should choose your mentors carefully. A Big Fish who is on the verge of bankruptcy or has turned to investors of last resort, i.e., Mexican drug cartels, is not the kind of Big Fish you want to be mentored by, unless you are interested in a career in organized crime.

Naturally, mentors are most important to the young networker who's just starting out on the economic climb. The choice of mentor is often the deciding factor that determines whether a young and ambitious person's dreams come true, especially if you are like most young people; i.e., in spite of your exalted place in the universe, your skill set is at best average.

The earlier one starts networking for a mentor, the better. If you are a member of that most disenfranchised caste of go-getters, the unpaid intern, know that networking a mentor for yourself early may be your only chance of surviving your first workplace experience.

Unless you obtained your internship through your parents, rich uncle, or other successful relative (in which case you're already a networker), whoever you are interning for will not simply treat you like a slave but will take pleasure in it. Why? Because that's how your boss was treated when he/she was an intern. Often, the abusive, annoying, and demeaning tasks that you, the intern, will be greeted with on that first day on the job will be due to the fact that your immediate superior got you, an intern to lighten their workload, rather than the pay raise or promotion they had been promised in their last job review.

How can the intern network beyond servitude? When your immediate master/mistress asks you to do unpleasant things, i.e., lick stamps, stay late photocopying graph paper, pick up lunch, fetch coffee, clean up coffee they deliberately drop, etc., always smile and offer a cheerful "No problem, I'll take care of it."

Why are you pretending to be happy? Because your immediate boss wants to break you. Your seemingly bottomless good humor and enthusiasm for drone work and humiliation will become more and more annoying to them. So annoying that your immediate boss, who is determined to crack you, will begin to create more and more elaborate fool's errands for you to run. In a matter of days they will have you picking up dry cleaning, walking the dog, purchasing condoms and/or sex aids, taking their urine sample to the lab, etc.

Now, as you set off on these fool's errands you are being forced to run, always make a point of purposely walking through that area of the workplace reserved for Big Fish. Stop any and all Big Fish you pass in the hall, or whose open office door provides an opportunity for face time, and volunteer, "I'm just dropping off Sally's urine sample, can I get you anything?" Which will in turn prompt the Big Fish to do one of two things: confront the employee you're interning for about using you to run personal errands, which will result in them firing you from a job you don't want anyway, or, more likely, inspire the Big Fish to put you to work running personal errands for him or her.

If the latter happens, do not mention this to your immediate superior. Tell the Big Fish who's above your boss on the corporate ladder that you are eager to learn as much about the business as possible and would "love" to come in on the weekends and help out. Soon, you will be changing the Big Fish's shelf paper at home. Babysitting their children. Washing their car. Which of course will lead the Big Fish to ask you to do things they would rather you not mention to your superior, their superior, or more important, their spouse. Soon you will be filling OxyContin prescriptions for them, getting them pot, helping them have an affair, etc. Once the Big Fish has trusted you with some detail of their life that would be embarrassing, you have succeeded in flipping the power dynamic of your work relationship.

Now if you are an intern and a networker and one of those readers who, in spite of our advice, intends to sleep his or her way to the top no matter what we say, your volunteer weekend work will offer you the perfect opportunity to give your future mentor the business.

> Remember, immediately after you have lost your office virginity, always act upset, morose, tearful. Wait until the Big Fish asks you at least twice what's wrong before answering. Trust us, the Big Fish you've just done the nasty with will be so relieved to hear that you aren't going to file a sexual harassment suit that you will only have to allude to the fact that you don't like the person you're interning for to prompt the Big Fish to do the right thing . . . for you. Follow our advice, and within twenty-four hours, you will have a paying job and an intern of your own to abuse.

As a networker, whether a lowly intern, Big Fish, or Whale, you are part of something much, much greater than the economic food chain; you are a part of what Lloyd Blankfein (CEO of Goldman Sachs) called a "virtuous cycle." Just as Blankfein sees the financial good deeds he performs for himself and others as "doing God's work," so should you. And remember, when the Almighty is at the top of your network, there's a special place in heaven waiting for you.

14

THE FAMILY THAT CLIMBS TOGETHER STAYS TOGETHER

One of the many joys of social climbing is that it is an activity the whole family can take part in.

> Teaching your children how to Mountaineer will not just give them the confidence and skills essential to leading a happy, healthy, and most important, rich life, it will bring your whole family closer together.

Single parent? Divorced? Not that we blame you, but social climbing with your children will teach them how to seek out friendships that will not only enrich their lives but also make them feel less lonely and disappointed that you couldn't hold on to your marriage.

To those Tiger Moms and Dads who say their children's lives are already overscheduled—violin lessons, tutors, soccer, hockey, basketball, etc.—get real. What are the odds your children are going to grow up and play the violin at Carnegie Hall?

Or get even a measly $10 million signing bonus for playing pro ball? Yes, if they achieve all-state status, those pastimes might help them get into one of the "right" universities. But if they tear their ACL, what happens to your family's dream? And even if they don't get hurt, they'll be so busy playing sports they won't have the free time or social skills to make the most of what going to a prestigious university is all about in the first place—forging friendships that can help them network and get a job after graduation that they otherwise wouldn't be able to get based on grades or talent.

Here are some basic tips that will help get you and your family climbing in the right direction—to the top!

When it comes to the arts and sciences of social climbing, New York City is the Athens of the twenty-first century. Climbing in the Big Apple isn't just a spectator sport that the whole city takes part in, it's a more fundamental ingredient in everyday life than any religion. A family doesn't put up with the cost, crime, and taxes of NYC if they are not aggressively and devoutly upwardly mobile. The same can be said to a lesser degree of life in any big city in America—Chicago, LA, San Francisco, Houston, Miami, Boston, etc.—but when it comes to climbing as a family, NYC is on the cutting edge. Because of this, seeing how it works in NYC will help you work it in your hometown.

The Right School

There are hundreds of private schools in New York City. Sadly, only a small fraction of them are considered the "right schools" and can truly help you and your child's climb. The yearly tuition at one of the right private nursery schools is more than twenty thousand dollars per year, and by the time your child is a teenager going to one of the right private high schools it will set you back in the neighborhood of forty grand per annum. All told, sending one child to one of the right schools from nursery through twelfth grade will cost you around half a million dollars. If that seems like a daunting number, know that you aren't just purchasing academic excellence, you are buying a lifetime's worth of social entrée for you and your child.

Of course, city climbers can send their child to one of the right boarding schools, too—Andover, Exeter, St. Paul's, Deerfield, etc.—they all provide an excellent education. But we feel Mountaineers who send their children away to boarding school are missing the opportunity to climb as a family. Yes, there are first-rate Mountaineering opportunities at elite boarding schools. You can take comfort in knowing your child will be bunking with the children of international tycoons, Chinese billionaires, European royalty, Russian oligarchs, and Third World dictators, at least one of whom will be destined to appear before a human rights tribunal. There's no question that giving your children an opportunity to make friends with the leaders of a country that lacks an extradition treaty might help them if they grow up to be a fugitive from justice. The question is, what will it do for you now?

Yes, on parent visiting days at boarding school, you will have the opportunity to meet exotic Big Fish and Whale parents of your child's friends. But even for the most rapid and audacious parent climber, there is so only so much Mountaineering that can be done in the course of a parents' weekend, especially when your hobnobbing opportunities are constantly being interrupted by meddlesome meetings with your child's teachers.

> The fun and payoff of sending your children to one of the right private day schools in New York City is that once they've been accepted at one of the right schools, you, as parents, will also be accepted, i.e., you will have the opportunity to meet Big Fish parents who can speed your climb every single day of the school year.

The parents of a child who attends one of these schools will find themselves at drop-off, pick-up, the school playground, athletic contests, etc., making small talk with billionaires, hedge fund princes, prize-winning novelists, Academy Award–winning actors, TV personalities, and diplomats, i.e., people whose bodyguards wouldn't let you get near them if their child weren't friends with your child on a daily basis. You won't ever have to ask Big Fish for their unlisted phone numbers, they're printed out in the school directory, along with the Big Fish's nickname . . . that's *if* your child gets into one of the right schools.

Think of all the exciting and profitable new best friends you could be making if your kid attended one of these elite institutions. You've read our chapter on networking; you know what to do once you're on a first-name basis with a Big Fish. From day one, admission to the right school will enable you and your children to step into the winner's circle together, and you will have the privilege of being able to social climb with them as you push their strollers into a better life.

After the pain of childbirth, the hours you've had to work Bugabooing your child from park to playground, not to mention the hours upwardly mobile mothers have had to work to afford the nanny to change the diapers and clean up the spit-up while they're at work, we say moms are entitled to get something for themselves from those bundles of joy that have given them stretch marks. Isn't it about time your offspring did something for you? Why should you have to do all the climbing?

Any psychologist will tell you it's not healthy for parents to hide the realities of life from their children: the hard work, the teamwork, and most important, the Mountaineering required to obtain the "good life." Get them into the right school and they'll understand Mommy and Daddy didn't get where they are by magic. Just as you had to climb, so will Junior.

Another advantage of sending your children to one of the right private day schools in the city, as opposed to a private boarding school, is that when the little ones come back to your apartment/home in the afternoon, you'll be able to coach and debrief them; teach them the subtle cues that will help five-year-olds determine whether they just had a playdate with a millionaire or a centimillionaire, i.e., a bona fide Whale. With a little help your first-grader will easily learn to recognize the difference between a Degas, a Picasso, a Lichtenstein, a Pollock, and a Basquiat, and will be able to tell you which of the kids in his/her class have such high-priced art hanging on their walls. By the time they are in second grade they will be able to ascertain whether the Monet water lilies above the fireplace is a seventy-nine-dollar print, or a $79 million oil. Do their playmate's mommy or daddy own the Lear Jet that flies them to Nantucket on weekends or is it just a NetJet? You know the questions they should be asking. And you will have the fun of teaching them the tricks of turning fun into ambition.

EMPOWERING THOUGHT #33

As a parent, think how much faster, easier, and more luxurious your family's climb would be if your son or daughter happened to overhear their best pal's mom and dad discussing the positive result of a drug trial at the pharmaceutical firm they work for. When a child innocently passes along information he or she happened to overhear, it's not insider trading; and even if it is, is the SEC really going to send your seven-year-old to jail?

Every major city in America has one or more of these right schools. In Houston, the greater percentage of the parents at one of the right schools will be in the oil/energy business. In Palo Alto, the young centimillionaire moms and dads will more than likely be computer geeks. And, of course, in Los Angeles, you'll have a higher percentage of parents in the entertainment business. Geography affects the makeup of the Big Fish parent population at the right schools, but one thing remains the same everywhere: Sadly, the best right schools for the upwardly mobile are invariably the ones that reject the most applicants.

Academic excellence is part of the sales pitch at every one of the right schools, regardless of where they're located. Glossy catalogs boast of second-graders learning Mandarin, Nobel Laureates lecturing fifth-grade science class, etc. But the real appeal, what the right schools are really selling, and the never-mentioned reason Big Fish, Whales, and famous and well-connected parents of every description want their children to go to these right schools is so their offspring will make friends with the children of even bigger Big Fish, bigger Whales, and even more famous and better-connected parents.

In a perfect world, everyone's children should and would be able to learn Mandarin in the second grade and have a Nobel Laureate lecture them in grade school. But the social climber knows the world is neither perfect nor fair.

Even if you can afford to spend what the average American family of four lives on in a year on your child's tuition, and even if your privileged tot's test scores surpass those of 97 percent of the other applicants, there's no guarantee your child will be accepted into this inner, über academic circle. In fact, the odds are against you. However, if you are a Big Fish/Whale, famous person, or "legacy" (a legacy meaning one of the child's parents attended the school themselves, which of course means that child has the advantage of being a second-generation social climber), these odds shift dramatically in your favor.

Each right school has its own selective and secretive

admissions policy. Though acceptance is never easy, the younger your children are when you apply, the easier it will be for them to get in. If you wait to fill out your first private school admissions forms until your child is going into the first grade, you and your progeny are sadly already behind the eight ball. How can that be? Because those applicants who have already attended the right feeder or nursery school will have preference over children whose parents were irresponsible enough to wait until they were six to start them social climbing.

What kind of networking/social climbing does it take to get into the high end of the food chain at age two and a half? Take the case of Mr. Jack Grubman. When he was a hot telecom stock analyst at Smith Barney, he wanted his twins to gain admission to the famed 92nd Street Y preschool. Around this time, he had also rated AT&T stock as "neutral," i.e., not a buy. Shortly after Grubman gave the unfavorable rating, he wrote a memorandum to Mr. Sandy Weill, then CEO of Citibank and a billionaire board member of AT&T, asking Sandy to help his children get into the 92nd Street Y preschool. According to *PBS Frontline*, Grubman wrote, "Given that it's statistically easier to get into the Harvard Freshman Class than it is to get into preschool at the 92nd Street Y [by the way, this is a correct statement], it comes down to 'who you know.'"

After writing this memo to Mr. Weill, Mr. Grubman upped his rating of AT&T from "neutral" to "buy." Which of course was good news for AT&T and Mr. Weill, who then contacted a member of the 92nd Street Y's board and recommended Mr. Grubman's children, who were soon accepted. Shortly after, a Citibank foundation then saw it in its heart to donate a million dollars to the 92nd Street Y preschool. Yes, Mr. Grubman has since been banned from the securities industry, but at least he got his children into one of the right schools.

To those who are saying to themselves, "Thank God that's not how it works at the right school in my town," wake up and smell the coffee. Also, think how much Mr. Grubman's children love him for what he taught them by example about climbing.

So how do parents who aren't analyzing and rating stocks get a Big Fish or Whale to go to bat for their children? Here's where love pays off in social climbing.

If you've been a great guest at a Big Fish's home for in excess of five years, have always laughed at their jokes, given them a jar of your bogus homemade jam at each and every visit, and most important, aided and abetted them or their spawn in avoiding disgrace, embarrassment, or arrest, you're in a good position to get a great letter of recommendation for your child.

Every social climber who has any thought of ever having children should early on identify and befriend any and all Big Fish they encounter who are on the board of one of the right schools in their city. Don't just make them your child's godparent. Name your firstborn after them. Help your child write them birthday and holiday cards. Encourage the little ones to call the Big Fish who can do the most for them Uncle and or Auntie.

> A word to the wise: It is always best to have the Big Fish give the letter of recommendation you have asked them to write to you and not send it directly to the school. Before forwarding a Big Fish's letter of recommendation to anything, always steam it open and read carefully. If the recommendation begins, "I have been asked to write a letter for . . ." do not send the letter. Why? To admissions committees to anything—school, club, or gated community—"I have been asked to recommend" is code for "this is the last person in the world you want to let in."

Never ask acquaintances or friends whose children have already gotten into the right school that you want your child to attend for help or advice concerning admissions. Why? Because they won't tell you the truth. Why? Because parents like to brag that their child did it all by themselves, and if they admit that their uncle donated a hockey rink or that their spouse affected the stock value of a board member's company, it will make their child seem less of a little genius.

To those upwardly mobile families who have gotten their progeny into a right school, congratulations! But know that your work has just begun. To take full advantage of the new climbing opportunities your child has opened up for you we suggest the following:

If your nanny is responsible for pick-up and drop-off, make sure that she understands that her Christmas bonus or help with her immigration problem is dependent on her setting up the right playdates. If your three-year-old and your nanny hang out with, say, a movie star's child and his/her nanny (Uma Thurman, Jerry Seinfeld, and Woody Allen all have children who attend one of NYC's right schools), chances are when Uma's, Jerry's, or Woody's kid has his/her birthday party, your child will be invited. In which case you, not your nanny, will bring your child to the birthday bash, ergo, you, having read our book, will soon find yourself friends with Uma, Jerry, or Woody.

Make up an excuse to casually drop into your child's private school and check the student signup sheets on the school bulletin board to find out whether the right parents are having their sons and daughters sign up for, say, tennis or baseball on the weekends. If the right sport turns out to be tennis and you have a son or daughter who loves baseball, gently explain to your child that if they make the wrong choice and decide to play the sport they like rather than the one you want them to, like tennis, they won't just be missing out on opportunities Mommy and Daddy worked hard to give them, they will also be making a mistake that could limit their future earning power. If that doesn't work, try bribery.

Summer, of course, means Mountaineering out of doors. Because the whole point of social climbing as a family is that all the boats in your little family's armada rise and fall together as one, we are against sending your child off for eight weeks to summer camp. Like boarding school, the camp experience does more to further your *child's* social ambitions than your own. Camp is also expensive. If you're already having trouble coming up with the private school tuition for your child or children, it's better value for the whole family to rent a summer house as close as you can afford to be to a beach, lake, or summer community where Big Fish swim. Or better yet, where Whales are known to surface.

It doesn't matter that you don't know any of the Whales or Big Fish that reside in your water hole of choice, or that you lack the extra scratch and entrée to belong to any of the right beach or country clubs. Send your seven-year-old over to the rich neighbor's house with a fresh-picked bouquet and your fruit compote, and the Big Fish (especially if they have no children or grandchildren of their own) will soon be inviting you and your seven-year-old over for dinner. If you and your family tag-team them with your well-rehearsed charm, it won't be long before they're inviting you to their beach/country club. Bear in mind: At most clubs each member can bring the same guest only four times per season, i.e., start using your child to endear yourself to their Big Fish friends ASAP.

As your children get older and your family matures, they will have more complicated social climbing decisions to make. If, for example, you're Jewish and your child's thirteenth birthday is approaching, you as a family will have to decide whether you can afford to throw a bat/bar mitzvah that won't embarrass you and your child. Yes, bar/bat mitzvahs are often as expensive as weddings, but given that a mediocre bar/bat mitzvah often gets you and your child invited to a great bar/bat mitzvah, we say go for it and hope that your child meets a future spouse at the event who has a trust fund large enough to benefit you and all your loved ones.

Nowadays, debutante parties are no longer an exclusively WASP tradition. Debutante parties present opportunities for the eighteen- to twenty-year-old daughters of social climbers of all races and religions to meet society spouses who can improve the cachet of the entire family. Compared to the cost of a bat/bar mitzvah, debutante parties are a bargain. In New York City there are three "coming out" galas: the International Debutante Ball and the Infirmary Ball, both held at the Waldorf Astoria, and the Junior Assemblies, held at the Pierre. All are by invitation.

The International sounds classier than it is. In point of fact, any young woman whose social climber parents can get their daughter to squeeze into elbow-length white kid gloves and a white ball gown that more often than not will make her look as large and poufy as a well-upholstered sofa and are willing to donate fourteen thousand dollars to the Soldiers', Sailors', Marines', Coast Guard and Airmen's Club can attend. Though a worthy charity, the International basically offers entrée to nothing but other social climbers. The Infirmary Ball, slightly larger and more exclusive, caters to a more metropolitan crowd and only requires a donation of seven thousand dollars. Think of it as the Lexus of debutante balls.

Though not all debutantes are WASPs, debutante parties are part of a WASP tradition that places as much value on frugality as it does on snobbery. In keeping with these values, the smallest, most exclusive ball of the season, the Junior Assemblies, is also the cheapest. It is so "exclusive" that the young ladies are not allowed to bring their grandparents, which is a much-appreciated blessing for those debutantes whose grandparents live in a trailer.

As Ms. Johnson knows from personal experience, though debutante parties are chaperoned, there are perils in sending one's daughter off to a ball in the Big City. She remembers wanting to use her debut to show her parents that she was a woman of the people, by opting to take the subway rather than their limo to the ball. An admirable inclination, but it was definitely a mistake to put on her ball gown and tiara and proceed to board a train that took her directly to Harlem. Parents should know that even the most docile of debutantes can make an unexpected wrong turn at any point in the evening.

> Though at any one of these events your daughter may in fact meet young men who will grow up to be billionaires, there are risks involved. Debutantes have a long history of becoming intoxicated, removing their ball gowns, doing fifty thousand dollars' worth of damage to their hotel suites, and/or getting knocked up by a busboy.

A membership in the right club may entail less risk than having your daughter become a debutante, but here, too, status comes with a price. Whether it be golf, golf and tennis, or tennis and beach, club membership can open up a whole new exciting world of climbing opportunities to your family. We will discuss the pros and cons of club membership and the admission process in detail in our chapter on Advanced Mountaineering. But for now, the basic questions you will be faced with are: a) Given that the initiation fee at one of the right clubs (the one that your child's friends at the right school belong to) is in the neighborhood of $250,000, can I afford to join? and b) Do I really want to belong to any club that would have me and my family as members?

EMPOWERING THOUGHT #34

There is no denying that climbing as a family will be more difficult for those who lack the disposable income necessary to pay for the right private schools, the right debutante balls, the right clubs, and the right bar/bat mitzvahs. But no matter what rung of the socioeconomic ladder you and your loved ones are on, one of you must know someone who has so much more of everything that you and your family member will be able to convince them to do the right thing, i.e., help you.

If you and your loved ones work as a team, you can flatter, charm, and manipulate that lonely old rich woman who lives down the block or on the other side of town into taking an interest in you and your children. Why? Because your local Big Fish, like everybody else in the world, need friends . . . even if they have to rent them.

To help you get a clear picture of where your family stands

with their social climbing, turn off the TV, shut down the computer, silence your iPhones, and sit down and have a serious conversation with your child, spouse, and yourself about how they can improve the prospects for the home team. Be open, honest, forthright, and responsible with your children. Compliment them on the important friendships they have already made and make a point of thanking them for getting their friend's dad to invite you to play golf at his club before reminding them that if they don't write better thank-you notes to Grandpa they might not get included in the will.

> Don't sugarcoat the truth—statistics show that adolescents actively involved in responsible social climbing have a far lower risk of drug abuse and unwanted teenage pregnancy.

15

SCENESTER SOCIAL CLIMBING

Scenester climbing is for all of you who would like to win friends, influence people, and get luxury goods conglomerates and vodka companies to pay for you to party 24/7/365. This method of Mountaineering is ideally suited for young adults birthed by baby boomers, otherwise known as Generation Y, who know they are special but have yet to do anything special.

To find out if you have what it takes to be a "scenester," ask yourself the following questions:

1. Are you a thrill seeker with a short attention span who feels entitled but isn't sure why?

2. Are you twenty-five years old, or can you pass for twenty-five in a dimly lit, crowded nightclub/trendy restaurant/hot bar, and do you like to hang out with Swans, supermodels, professional athletes, rap stars, or Big Fish from the worlds of fashion, finance, and film?

3. Do you enjoy alcohol and/or drugs, especially if someone else is paying for them?

4. Do you have the stamina and discipline to stay up until five in the morning, night after night after night, to catch a whiff of fresh-brewed zeitgeist?

5. Do you own a hoodie, not like to shave every day, or look good in black and not have a job to get up and go to in the morning?

6. Do you lack the skills, inclination, cognitive ability, or the attention deficit medication to actually sit down and do something creative but still consider yourself a creative person?

7. Are you the kind of upwardly mobile youngish person who believes that an essential ingredient for a meaningful life is knowing and doing what is hip, hot, sick, next wave, cutting edge, and au courant when it comes to nightspots, tattoos, piercings, bikini waxes, Third World condiments, the latest fashion in orthopedically damaging footwear prescribed in Paris, and other such subjects, so you can say "been there, done that" a week before the rest of the world reads about them in the blogosphere?

8. And most important, do you have the courage to be deeply, truly, and successfully superficial?

If you answered yes to any one of the above, then scenester climbing just might be the right method of Mountaineering for you. Obviously, scenester climbing will work best for those readers who live in a city where there actually are hot nightclubs, fashionable restaurants, and trendy bars. Not that we at *The Social Climber's Bible* are geographical snobs, but in the VIP section at the trendiest, hottest hotspots in Scranton, Shreveport, or Urbana, you will be unlikely to find a person who's ever shared a toilet seat with a Swan, "It" girl, rap star, celebrity athlete, famous actress, movie director, or artist, much less someone who's actually met a certified member of the twenty-first-century after-dark demimonde.

The good news for the millions of you who live in or near nightlife capitals of the world like New York, Los Angeles, Miami, Las Vegas, London, Paris, Berlin, and Hong Kong is that at eleven o' clock tonight your time, in whatever time zone you live in, there are establishments open to the public that will be teeming with glamorous Big Fish, reigning celebrities, and happening somebodies who can change your life.

Want to meet them? Of course you do. The question is, how *much* do you want to meet them?

The names of these nighttime venues for personal advancement are not secret. If you've been doing your homework and keeping up with the gossip columns, nightlife blogs, and party pics online, you should know about them already. You should also know that the hottest spot on the planet in New York or Paris or Shanghai at this very moment will not be the hottest spot on the planet six months from now. And sadly, eight months after that it will be a watering hole for the bridge-and-tunnel set.

For example, in late 2012, the hip social climber in NYC would have found scenester celebrities and avant-garde Big Fish lurking in nightclubs like Acme (downstairs, of course) and the

Electric Room. The year before that, it was all about the Beatrice Inn.

We know what you're thinking: If these ultra-hot spots full of cool, trendoid Big Fish are open to the public, why doesn't every social climber go there? Because, though legally they are open to the public, they are in fact every bit as exclusive, restrictive, elitist, and discriminating in their admissions policies, dress and decorum codes, etc., as those legendarily impossible-to-get-into old-money WASP country clubs.

The grooveball establishment of the moment is no less snobbish and status conscious than the most bigoted of old-school clubs. They're just snobbish and bigoted about different things. Though the criteria for admission to California's Bohemian Grove club and, let's say, French nightlife impresario and graffiti artist André Saraiva's new downtown New York club, Le Baron, are totally different in terms of dress code and status accessories required for entrée, they are identical in that their primary appeal stems from the fact that they are both nearly impossible to get into.

As the *New York Observer* boasted, Monsieur Saraiva's Le Baron would "offer the tightest door since the Beatrice Inn in its heyday." In other words, its success and desirability depend on keeping people like you out.

The nightclub doorman serves the same purpose as the admissions committee of the country club. Their job is to deny entry to those who don't belong, the wannabe scenester as opposed to the real scenester. Exclusivity has evolved since the days of Studio 54 and its famed velvet rope. Today, the choicest nightspots have no sign or name on the door to identify them. A mob of wannabes waiting for entrée that may never be granted by the doorman is the only advertisement a truly cool establishment needs. Though the velvet rope is gone, the doorman still reigns supreme, and note: The doorman, even if she is a woman, is invariably aimed with a three-hundred-pound bouncer at his side, who looks like he shared a cell with 50 Cent, on guard to make sure the un-Chosen take no for an answer and make way for the Chosen People of the night.

The challenge for the scenester social climber is to become one of the Chosen People.

The keepers of the gate are naturally partial to young Big Fish businessmen willing to spend four hundred dollars for a twenty-eight-dollar bottle of vodka. Why are Big Fish willing to do that? In part because demonstrating that they can buy happiness makes them feel better about what they had to do to get the money they're burning. But the real attraction for Big Fish doesn't stem from the fact that they get pleasure from being grossly overcharged for a bottle of vodka. What excites them is that overpaying for vodka enables them to sit in the VIP section next to people who *are* officially hip because they are in the business of being cool.

EMPOWERING THOUGHT #35

Paying four hundred dollars for a twenty-eight-dollar bottle of vodka and rubbing up next to scenesters, as opposed to lap dancers, in a hot, crowded club makes Wall Street Big

> Fish feel hip and cool, two qualities they know
> they lack but hope will rub off on them if they
> get drunk and/or sweaty enough.

Who besides Big Fish with obscene amounts of money do doormen think are officially cool? Fashion designers, magazine editors, artists, movie stars, directors, supermodels, professional athletes, etc. Given that you are probably neither a Big Fish nor genuinely hip, talented, creative, or a beautiful ingredient in the zeitgeist, how do you get the doorman to let *you* inside so you can be misperceived by the Big Fish and the officially "hip" as being a bona fide scenester?

To begin with, you have to look right to the doorman. Here's where the hoodies, not shaving every day, and liking to wear black come in. The successful scenester's wardrobe is never flamboyantly flashy, inventive, or overly chic. That's for the club kids who have a genuine sense of style. What you as a social climber and would-be scenester possess is a strategy and a willingness to do whatever it takes to get to the top, i.e., to risk humiliation.

Your clothes should be utilitarian/workmanlike. As if being authentic is your job. What you wear isn't as important as how you wear it.

> The scenester isn't just casually rumpled; the scenester doesn't believe in ironing. It is not the costume, but the attitude you must wear that will get you past the doorman of the hottest club on the planet.

So while you think about that, put on your hoodie, stand in front of the mirror, and let's work on your look. A scenester has a seen-it-all glaze to his/her expression. Your eyes don't twinkle, they never did, even when you were a kid. Most of all, you're never surprised. As you breathe, try to imagine you're exhaling all your feelings; you are unfazed, neutral about everything, including yourself and your insecurities. The effect you want is the postmodern equivalent of contentment, otherwise known as boredom.

EMPOWERING THOUGHT #36

Even if you are not capable of "trying hard," looking as if you are not trying hard is hard work.

If you are a scenester, you do not smile, you smirk. Not in a dismissive way, but as if you were the only one in the world who realizes the joke is on the universe. Model your facial expressions on David Carradine's. Not when he accidentally strangled himself while practicing autoerotic asphyxiation in a closet in Bangkok, but back when he was on TV playing Kwai Chang Caine in *Kung Fu*.

If you, in spite of our mantra, still find yourself haunted by those shaming and judgmental spirit killers, parents, school principals, and high school guidance counselors who wrote you off as the underachiever's underachiever, you will be glad to know that your lack of success in the real world will give you a leg up when climbing the alternative ladder of hipness. Previous personal failures and permanent blemishes on your record that would hold you back if you were a conventional social climber will actually work to your advantage in the scene of the scenester.

As with all aspects of social climbing, the key to personal success is turning your negatives into positives simply by having the courage to "flip it." If you were kicked out of high school, particularly if you were expelled from one of the right schools, don't hide it; brag about it. Don't mention that you were thrown out for cheating or eating paste in the ninth grade, say you set the gym on fire because you needed it for a scene in a film you were shooting.

Take a page from James Frey, and his best-selling quasi-bogus memoir *A Million Little Pieces*. Make stuff up about yourself, not cool good stuff but cool bad stuff, that makes you seem like a genuine, one-of-a-kind rebel without a cause as opposed to what you really are, a social climber who lives in the city and doesn't have a regular job or own an iron. If you had a misdemeanor on your record for possessing a joint, blow it up into a story that will convince the demimonde in the VIP section that even though you have less to show for your life than they do, you have lived more.

Confabulate a bad girl/bad boy past in an exotic locale that involves smuggling heroin and/or a stint in a Third World war zone and/or prison. Even though you still haven't gotten into the nightclub, you will have to have your badass backstory ready. Play your cards right and there is a chance that someone who's officially hip inside the club—a magazine publisher, movie star, or director—will buy your life rights. And then you'll not only be officially hip but also famous for being hip.

But before any of those things can happen you have to get past the doorman. The trouble is, having a look, attitude, act, and backstory that will impress the people inside will not impress the doorman until you have been deemed officially hip by one of the trendoid Big Fish inside. Which of course can't happen if you can't get past the doorman.

How do you break the vicious Catch-22 of cooldom that faces every scenester when starting out? Lurk on the edge of the crowd of wannabes who are clamoring to get in. Do not make eye contact with the doorman. Stand apart from the crowd by one of the double-parked limos as if you just got out of it and are meeting some friends who need your help to get into the club/restaurant/bar. Granted, this method might require you to spend several nights in the gutter outside the club of choice, but eventually, if you're persistent, you will see your ticket in.

What is your ticket in? At least once a week, every big-city late-night coolest place to be on the planet is approached by a posse of underage revelers who are in a position to change the course of the scenester's social life. What gives them this power? They are the spawn of name-brand Whales. By Whale, think Trump, Rothschild, Kennedy, Bush, etc., the jailbait sons and daughters of bankable movie stars, or the offspring of hedge fund kings and nationally elected officials. If you have been following our advice and preparing for this moment by studying society pages, you will recognize them. We will go into the many peculiarities of Whales later, but for now, what you need to know is that Whale spawn are almost always startlingly naïve about the power their last name holds over doormen. And if by chance this is the junior Whale's first outing to the hottest place on the planet sans Mommy and Daddy Whale, and you are camped out in the gutter waiting for them, you just might be in a position to change your position on the planet. The junior Whales of mega somebodies, especially if they are nightlife virgins, will be uncertain how to get into the club. In six months, they will be jaded enough to show no restraint in flaunting their last name. But if you spot them as they take their first staggering steps in the long, elegant pub crawl that in most cases will be their life's journey, there is a good chance they will still be under the quaint misperception that there is something unhip/not cool about dropping Daddy's/Mommy's name in public to get what they want. Which of course is where you come in. While the junior Whales armed with fake IDs are working up the courage to announce themselves to the doorman, step forward.

Be careful not to look as if you're trying to jump the line, lest the doorman sic his bouncer on you. *Now* is the time to make eye contact with the doorman. Give him the smirk you've been practicing in the mirror and whisper, "Mr. Trump/Lord Rothschild [or whoever] was hoping his son/daughter wouldn't have to wait too long to get in." Nod toward the junior Whales who are huddled together at the edge of the crowd as if they are with you. Now the doorman might or might not recognize them, but he certainly won't recognize you. And even if he can't place the teenage faces, or see the resemblance, he will note that they are very expensively dressed for teenagers. And the sight of a sixteen-year-old with a diamond-encrusted platinum Rolex, or an eleven-thousand-dollar Chanel purse, will tell him that inside that purse is a black AmEx, which means that even though they're underage, they're sure to buy a thousand dollars' worth of drinks. Plus, the doorman will know there are perks that come from doing a solid for Mommy and Daddy Whale/Mega Somebody.

The doorman will of course wonder who you are. Do you work for Papa Whale? Are you a friend of Mama Whale? Are you Papa Whale's scenester stepbrother? And while the doorman is wondering all that, turn your smirk on the Whale children and beckon them to follow you in a way that will make them think that it was you who got them past the doorman, rather than their own last names. As you graciously let the Whale spawn and his or her friends proceed ahead of you, give the doorman the hipster's combo of handshake half squeeze and back pat, what we call the "I'm in the club hug," and say, "It's always good to see you again."

Because all scenesters look more or less the same, the doorman will not only think that you are in some cool way connected to the Whale whose name you dropped but think that he has also let you into the club before, i.e., that you have already been deemed officially cool.

To push your advantage, catch up to the Whale's son or daughter and their friends, and volunteer, "Sorry that took so long, that doorman can be a real dick." Now you are not only friends with the doorman, you are friends with the Whale spawn and their friends, who are under the false impression that you have an intimate connection to the hottest club on the planet.

Repeat your story about Daddy Whale hoping their daughter/son won't have to wait too long to get a table to the guardian of the VIP section and you will soon be sitting in a banquette next to rap stars, professional athletes, supermodels, Swans, magazine editors, etc. And as the Whale's daughter/son begins to buy four-hundred-dollar bottles of twenty-eight-dollar vodka and you teach her/him how to table dance, you will be an official scenester.

On subsequent nights, reconnect with the Whale child and his/her posse outside the other hottest places on the planet—restaurants that require an unlisted number to make a reservation and bars that aren't officially opened unless you are a somebody. You, of course, simply by showing up and dropping Papa Whale's name, will make the doors open and a table magically appear. Be avuncular and protective, i.e., make out with the Whale spawn, but do not sleep with them, and their posse will become your posse. In two weeks, it will be your name that makes the doormen open the gates to opportunity.

Of course, while squiring junior Whales about town on their credit cards, there's one possibility the scenester must be prepared for. In the unlikely event you enter a nightclub with the spawn and happen to encounter Mama or Papa Whale, do not panic. Greet them as if you've already met them. As always, say, "It's good to see you again." Tell them you came to this club specifically because you heard they were there. If their children say that's a lie, tell Mama and Papa their child's teasing them. Insist that the maître d' set up a special table, tell the senior Whales what a wonderful job they're doing raising their child, order a round of vodka shots, and get the whole family table dancing.

No question, if all of the above happens, in a few short months you will be NBFs with junior *and* senior Whales and "officially hip" at all the super trendy nightclubs, bars, and restaurants you have been frequenting six nights a week. It will be clear to all that your evenings are spent being what you are, a scenester.

WARNING

Eventually the subject of what you do during the day besides sleep is bound to come up.

Though you realize that if you had a steady day job you would never have been able to spend your evenings waiting to befriend a pod of underage Whales and gain the entrée you deserved, ironically and unfairly those genuinely accomplished hipster Big Fish, rap stars, supermodels, etc., who you are now spending your evenings with will be inclined to think that a twenty-five-year-old who goes out every night, doesn't have a day job, and gets rich kids to pay for his drinks is a low-life barfly. Hence it is best to establish early on a more socially acceptable explanation for your lifestyle, i.e., start telling people that you are a "conceptual artist."

Why a "conceptual" artist? Because if you said you were a painter, they'd ask to see your paintings. Or if you told them you were a writer, they'd want to read your work. If asked to describe or show your conceptual art, tell them you are working on a performance piece about "identity"—which is sort of true. If they ask where they can see this conceptual artwork, tell them that you're having a one-man/-woman show at Helsinki's Museum of Contemporary Art in eight months and promise to invite them. Do not worry, eight months in a scenester's life is the equivalent of eight years of an average human existence.

Now that you have a cool professional passion, i.e., a good excuse for being a barfly, it's time for you to find a cool way to make money. Because you are now seen everywhere and know everyone, and are buds with all the Big Fish who like to spend four hundred dollars on twenty-eight-dollar bottles of vodka, as well as the Whales who are cool because they are Whales, plus those who are officially cool because they actually do something cool, and most important because you have kept track of all their email addresses and unlisted phone numbers, the owners of those clubs and restaurants and their competitors who are opening newer and hotter nightclubs, bars, and restaurants will want you to invite all your new happening best friends to their establishment. And because you are a struggling conceptual artist, you will be able to get away with charging them for that service without seeming usurious.

Soon, you will be getting paid to make sure your Whales, Big Fish, rap stars, supermodels, professional athletes, and fashionista friends show up at the opening of every new nightclub, restaurant, and hot spot in town. It won't be long before you will own a percentage of one or more of these establishments. Fashion designers will give you free clothes to wear. You will get paid to be the nonmodel model hipster in Gap ads that mention you are a conceptual artist. Brands of vodka and tequila that come in bottles that look like Mayan artifacts will put you on a retainer to serve only their intoxicants and to always be photographed with a Mayan bottle at your lips. You are now not just a person who's officially cool, you're a celebrity brand.

Because by this time several months will have passed and your nonexistent conceptual art show in Helsinki will be approaching, it is time for you to have the PR firm that now manages your ever-expanding popularity issue a press release. It will state that as a conceptual artist you realized that the whole notion of a museum exhibition of your work is an outmoded nineteenth-century concept, and you've decided the only way you can stay true to your artistic sensibilities is to do something that is both new, socially conscious, and profit-making. Announce that you are opening up your own nightclub. And because you are environmentally as well as socially aware, it will be entirely green in its construction and libations, a place where like-minded people can talk about ways to make the world a better place—a chain of emporiums of good vibes and love, the flagship of which will be built in Las Vegas and named after yourself.

Not only is all of the above within a scenester's grasp, stay friends with the junior Whales that first allowed you to get your foot in the door, past the doorman, and up the ladder, and ten, twenty years down the line, when you're no longer hip or young, and are most likely fat and balding but very, very rich, with spoiled spawn of your own, you can go to those now middle-aged Whales, reminisce about how you got them into their first nightclub, and they'll agree to write your child a well-deserved letter of recommendation to get him or her into the right nursery school.

16

THE AARP CLIMB: WHY CLIMBING GETS EASIER THE OLDER YOU GET, EVEN IF YOU WEAR DEPENDS

One of the greatest things about social climbing is that there's no mandatory retirement age. You can do it until the day you die. If you are sixty-five-plus and are just starting to climb, don't kick yourself for all those decades you spent hiding in the closet, ashamed of your upwardly mobile urges—get out there and start making the kinds of friends you've always wanted and deserved. If you've spent your life raising a family, tell them they're on their own. It's time for Grandma/Grandpa to look out for Grandma/Grandpa.

For those seniors who have been Mountaineering their whole lives and fear that they've reached their peak, know that if you follow the tips in this chapter, your best years of climbing will still be ahead of you.

EMPOWERING THOUGHT #37

There's no such thing as an old social climber. Think of yourself as a Stradivarius violin—the older the fiddle, the sweeter the tune.

The golden years offer Mountaineers opportunities that weren't open to them when they were twenty-five. Admittedly, scenester social climbing might be challenging for those over sixty-five, but for those upwardly mobile seniors blessed with a great plastic surgeon, a state-of-the-art hearing aid, and a divorce settlement from an extremely wealthy ex-spouse, nothing is impossible; we say go for it. For inspiration, check out forever-young septuagenarian Jocelyn Wildenstein, ex-wife of Alec Wildenstein, billionaire French businessman, art dealer, and racehorse owner. Yes, her face now looks as if it belongs to a cat, but she definitely doesn't look seventy-four.

Even if you have kept your own face, the rules have changed since you started climbing; the old guard hasn't just let down their guard, they're dying off. Ladders you were prohibited from climbing in your youth are now open to you. Best of all, the senior social climber who is only now returning to the circuit will be happy to discover that a great many of the snobs who snubbed you or deliberately prevented you from feeling comfortable reaching for the higher rungs of the ladder are now too infirm or senile to bust you for embellishing your past with accomplishments, famous friends you never had, etc.

In other words, no matter what your station in life, at this moment, you will have a much-deserved, ever-increasing freedom to become new best friends with a whole new class of Big Fish. All you have to do is turn off the TV, get off the couch, put in your dentures, and start sucking up to the right people.

While the rest of your generation is retiring, it's time for you to get to work. Demographics, median income, and the appeal of warm winter weather will naturally lead many of you to the gilded retirement enclaves of Florida's Gold Coast, Palm Beach, or better yet, Hobe Sound, where the notoriously strict dress codes were written to make every woman on the island look over sixty. According to local legend, if a young woman wore a dress that was deemed too revealing, a black sweater would be left on her porch indicating she was no longer welcome at the club. Others of you may prefer those gated desert oases of golf, yoga, and spa fun—Taos, Palm Springs, etc. Whether you're flying off to warmer climes for the first time or already have a toehold in a community populated by oldie Big Fish, know this: They need you more than you need them. Old Big Fish have to lower their standards if they want to hang out with people who are still living, which means that as long as you are not hooked up to a respirator, you can still be the life of the party.

EMPOWERING THOUGHT #38

Because male Big Fish die a decade before female Big Fish, the extra man, even if he is a very old man, is always in demand; any single

> senior Mountaineer who has the manners to
> chew with his mouth closed, is vaguely hetero-
> sexual, and still has his prostate is a total catch
> in the henhouse of retirement life.

Admittedly, the upwardly mobile woman of sixty-five-plus will be somewhat less popular than the senior male of the species. But Mountaineers of either sex who have the imagination to keep up both sides of the conversation while they push the wheelchair of a senior Big Fish who's recovering from a stroke can become best friends with the person who snubbed them forty years ago.

If you're a member of the AARP set and just starting to climb, the same advice we gave the young social climber back in Chapter 1 applies to you. Start by standing in front of the mirror and appraising your assets. Because we don't want you to be shocked, do not take off all your clothes; underwear will suffice.

> If you're an oldie who's frightened by what you see, remember: The average sixty-year-old looks hot to any person who's over the age of ninety, especially if he or she is suffering from glaucoma.

If that doesn't cheer you up, remember, our mantra applies every bit as much to you as it does to the twenty-year-old who's reading this book:

I CARE ENOUGH ABOUT ME NOT TO BELIEVE

ANYTHING THEY SAY ABOUT ME IS TRUE IF I DON'T WANT IT TO BE. I WILL NOT BE JUDGED.

For those of who are still depressed by what you see in the mirror and want to think about investing in plastic surgery before you start climbing, we suggest you put your clothes back on and consider the following. Contrary to what one might assume, our research shows that for the senior female Mountaineer, looking younger doesn't make you climb faster. In fact, new breasts and body-lifts can work to your detriment. Why? Because if you are as wrinkled as a white raisin, the Big Fish widow who has had so many lifts her face now resembles a raw chicken shrouded in cling wrap won't see you as competition.

If you look natural, i.e., your actual age, she will think she looks better in comparison, and will be more likely to invite you to stay with her for extended periods of time. She'll fly you south, give you your own guest cottage on her estate, and insist you tag along to parties and galas to make it less obvious that she is trolling for her third, fourth, or fifth husband.

The shrewd, mature female Mountaineer knows that by looking and acting her actual age, she will be far less likely to be labeled as a social climber. Let your hair go gray, take up yoga, and most important, profess a deep belief in reincarnation. Aging Big Fish are cheered by the possibility they will come back as a Whale.

If you have your own fears about mortality, keep them to yourself. Instead of debating what hymn you want played at your funeral or angling to get a plot in a restricted cemetery, cheer yourself and everyone else up with a few wild stories about affairs you never had in your twenties with the likes of John Lennon, Norman Mailer, or Wilt Chamberlain. Older male Big Fish will be fighting to have you as their dinner partner if you can talk dirty about the dead. If asked by someone who has known you for forty years why you never revealed these triple-X-rated celebrity liaisons before, simply smile and say that your late husband was an extremely jealous man. Because rheumatoid arthritis and artificial joints make it harder for old people to do dirty things, they appreciate hearing about them. Remember, the greatest of all the great things about senior social climbing is that senility gives you an excuse for any and all social blunders you may make—be bold, reckless, but don't break a hip.

The rules are different for the male Mountaineer over sixty. For you the climb is more of a beauty contest. As such, those older male readers who could benefit from a tummy tuck, liposuction, or breast reduction should consider surgically lightening their load before beginning their ascent. Yes, it will be painful, but think of the thrill of victory you will experience when the widow of that Big Fish who blackballed you from the golf club or made you feel like a loser for not getting into Harvard fifty years ago invites you to borrow her dead Big Fish husband's golf clubs, or better yet, invites you to lie down in his bed for a "nap."

The same basic rules we laid out for the young social climber—flattery will get you everywhere, the importance of being a great guest, etc.—all apply to older Mountaineers, except when it comes to sex. Let's be honest, if you're over sixty, you're no longer playing the long game. If you've still got it in you, *now* is the time to sleep your way to the top! Even if you can't actually have sex.

Worried you aren't what you used to be in the sack? Even if the sex is less than satisfactory, one or both of you will be so relieved that you were actually able to have sex that it won't seem unsatisfactory. And in the unlikely event that the sex is actually great for the Big Fish, she, unlike the younger version of herself, won't be able to do it again and again and again. Cut your Viagra with Celebrex and you will be in and out of the sack and back on the golf course or at the bridge table at her club in no time, freeing you up to network into the hearts of her even bigger old Big Fish friends.

If you are escorting a widow, do not try to compete with the dead. Speak well of the widow's ex, even if she herself trashes her late spouse, and it will make you seem like a bigger person than you are. If the Big Fish widow is still grieving and starts to cry at the mention of her lost loved one, wrap your arms around her and comfort her with a hug. Do not use this moment of bereavement to immediately stick your tongue down her throat. Instead, think of something sad—your dog dying when you were twelve, or the alimony you're paying your wife—something that will help you squeeze out a few genuine tears of your own. Whisper, "I'm so sorry for your loss," let her have a good cry, and then cop a cheap feel.

The same advice we gave young social climbers applies to you regarding the opportunities to be gained by attending memorial services, AA meetings, art gallery openings, etc. But you should also take advantage of those opportunities for making new best friends that are only open to the AARP set. Linger in your cardiologist's waiting room and strike up a conversation with the septuagenarian who has a new pacemaker and a winter home in Palm Beach. Loiter on the wheelchair ramp at the poshest physical rehabilitation facility in your town and chat up the hot old Big Fish babe with the walker. Remember, it's easier to use the Velcro-Climber technique with someone who can't walk, much less run, away from you.

> Rich, famous, and powerful people who are getting older need new friends. Especially when their children are eager to dump them into an assisted-living village.

You can make the difference in the quality of their final years—and yours. Convincing them that instead of selling their beach house or second, third, or fourth home and giving that money to their greedy children, they should get another season's worth of fun out of it and invite you to spend the summer or winter with them. Even if your new best decrepit Big Fish friend passes on before the season's over, sad as you feel, there's always the chance you'll find out that your old pal showed his or her appreciation for your loyal friendship by leaving that beach house to you.

Of course, there's no denying that senior citizen social climbers have their own health issues to worry about. Remember, part of being an older great guest is being able to listen to your aging Big Fish friends complain about their aches and pains, while never giving in to the temptation to kvetch about the parts of your own body that need replacement. If you're a "walker" who can't keep up or starts falling down, get a walker. And remember . . . if, God forbid, you have a heart attack while your host/hostess is giving a party, have the good manners to do it quietly and think of the bright side. If you survive, chances are your host/hostess will feel so guilty, they invite you to convalesce in their retirement home in the style you, by now, have become accustomed to.

17

RIDING UNICORNS AND WHALES

The single most important individual in a social climber's life, other than themselves of course, are members of that rare breed who, due to a combination of talent, influence, and newsworthy achievement, possess a kind of celebrity that has such magical properties their celebrity status rubs off on those around them. The climber who is smart and lucky enough to become their friend not only gets to enjoy the perks and privileges normally accorded to those who have done something extraordinary, he or she also gets to enjoy the thrill of being semifamous for simply having become the friend of someone who's genuinely famous.

Whereas a Big Fish or, better yet, a Whale can give you a huge boost up the ladder, friendship with one of these game changers can beam you up to a universe where everyone is a somebody. Because of the magical effect they can have on a social climber's life, we like to think of game changers as "Unicorns."

Neither money nor fame nor power nor beauty nor talent

alone make someone a Unicorn. A Unicorn's good fortune must come in multiples. For example, the Clintons, George Clooney, Angelina Jolie, Jay Z, Beyoncé, Prince William, Anna Wintour, and Sir Paul and Stella McCartney are certified Unicorns. The alchemy of that Holy Trinity of accomplishment, power, and bold-faced fame makes Unicorns sexy even if they're totally lacking in sex appeal. Examples: Henry Kissinger and Chelsea Clinton.

Movie stars and directors of movies that gross over $500 million worldwide or have won an Oscar are Unicorns until they have three flops in a row. However, celebrities like Angelina Jolie and Bono have lifetime status as game changers because they not only have fame and fortune and sex appeal, they are also professional do-gooders. All ex-presidents are Unicorns, except Jimmy Carter, who lacked Unicorn status even when he was president. Madonna still thinks she is a Unicorn, because her friends are afraid to tell her that she's not.

Unicorns' status is relative and can have geographical limitations. For example, if you live in Minneapolis, becoming new best friends with the local legendary Purple Unicorn, Prince, or pals with Zygi Wilf, owner of the Minnesota Vikings, will make you the toast of Minneapolis. However, the magic of those friendships will get you invited to little more than the grand opening of a Taco Bell in LA or New York.

For those who think they don't have a snowball's chance in hell of ever knowing the excitement and unearned access that comes to those who have the good fortune to hitch a ride to the top on the back of a Unicorn, ponder this: Since every one of the aforementioned Unicorns is surrounded by social climbers, why not you? There's always room for one more hanger-on.

Remember, because of the fame factor, their high-profile public persona, Unicorns are far more skittish than Whales. They should never be approached directly.

Whereas Big Fish and Whales are suckers for blatant flattery, Unicorns are so used to being fawned over that direct praise will raise the short hairs on the back of their necks and send them running. Your garden variety of suck-up compliment, "I loved your last movie," "My son/daughter wrote a history report about you," "I can't believe I'm meeting you," "What's it like to win the Nobel Prize?" is as much of a social no-no as asking a major league ballplayer to autograph your genitalia.

Unicorns already have fans: You are a social climber, not a fan. As such, you should know what the Unicorn needs and lacks is a friend like *you*—a Mountaineer equipped with the wit, charm, and self-confidence to make the Unicorn believe that you are attracted to them as a person, not the bold-faced name they worked so hard to become.

The narcissism of the Unicorn is paradoxical. The need to be special, which coupled with talent makes them special, also eventually and inevitably makes them feel they're so extra-special that they're entitled to be both special and normal at the same time. Though this is physically impossible, it does open the door for Unicorn–social climber friendships. Make Unicorns feel that they are normal. Pretend to be immune to their magic, oblivious to their superstar status, and they will be the ones who will be pursuing you for friendship.

EMPOWERING THOUGHT #39

The trick to befriending celebrities, aka Unicorns, is making them think they have singled you out for friendship because you, unlike 99.99 percent of the rest of the world, treat them as if they are normal, when in fact you have been stalking them for years.

How does one get close enough to a Unicorn to give them the false impression that they are a normal person and you are unfazed by the magical powers that come from their Unicorn status?

If you live in a major city and have done your homework, you will eventually succeed in social climbing your way, via a Big Fish, to a charity gala and/or a Whale party where the invite will indicate a Unicorn will be the guest of honor. Do not be intimidated. Remember that none of the above-mentioned game changers started out life as a Unicorn.

Rupert Murdoch, at the age of twenty-one, was an Australian Turtle. Jacqueline Bouvier Kennedy Onassis was just another Swan until she hooked JFK.

Remind yourself, Unicorns are just like you in that they have to put their trousers on one leg at a time, even if they do have someone on staff to tie their shoelaces.

As always, planning is the key to making a success of your first encounter with a Unicorn. Say, for the purpose of this exercise, you have wangled a Big Fish into inviting you to a World Wildlife Fund charity event at which Bill Clinton and Angelina Jolie are being honored. Naturally, as a social climber, you would love to get to know Bill and/or Angelina. Fat chance of that happening, unless you think out of the box when it comes to your conversation starter.

Just as a professional soccer player might feign a limp to put an opponent off guard, you need to make a move that will shift the game in your favor. For example, before you put on your tux or dress, apply a large bandage to your calf if you're a man and to your thigh if you're a woman. Now dab a bit of ketchup on the bandage as if you have a leaking wound. Make no mention of your imaginary injury to anyone you are sitting with at the party.

When you see Bill and/or Angelina or whatever Unicorn you're stalking being bored by less cunning social climbers than yourself, approach the feeding frenzy with a limp—but do not make eye contact with the Unicorn. When you are within three feet of the Unicorn, stop short and wince in seemingly excruciating pain. Now, still ignoring the Unicorn, raise the pant leg of your tuxedo or the hem of your dress and expose the bandage.

Unicorns like to show off the fact that along with having more talent, influence, and celebrity than mere mortals, they also possess a superior sense of empathy when it comes to the suffering of non-Unicorns. Nine times out of ten, the sight of your wound and your obvious discomfiture will prompt curiosity and concern, especially if they are bored with the conversation they are having and looking for a way out.

Now, if you are a woman displaying a bandaged thigh to a Unicorn like Bill Clinton, chances are you will have to do little else to get his immediate and undivided attention. But even as skittish a Unicorn as Angelina Jolie will not be able to resist an opportunity to show her superior empathy by taking the time to ask you some version of the following: "What happened to your leg?"

At which point, you will stop wincing and answer casually, "I got bit by a baby cheetah I was rescuing from a poacher's trap on the Serengeti."

No matter what they think of your legs, the odds are that neither Angelina nor Bill will have encountered anyone suffering so noble a wound, at least not in the last twenty-four hours. Hence, the Unicorn is going to be impressed, sympathetic, and interested enough to ask you who you are. Resist the temptation to give the Unicorn your last name. Only give your first name.

This will make them charmed and curious, and most important, put you on equal footing. They will then introduce themselves. Which is something Unicorns haven't had to do in so long, they will get a kick out of saying their own name. When they ask what you were doing in the Serengeti rescuing the baby cheetah, simply say, "I'm an accountant/yoga instructor/insurance salesperson who likes animals."

They will think you are being modest and then invite you over to their table so you can tell Brad Pitt/Hillary Clinton about saving the cheetah. Important: Keep the cheetah story to a minimum. Talk about the boring details of your own life. How the bloodstains from your nonexistent baby cheetah bite have ruined three pairs of pants/dresses and the dry-cleaning bill is cleaning you out, i.e., discuss things they used to talk about before they became Unicorns. If you remind them of the person they used to be before they became magical, they will like you. Why? Not because you saved a cheetah, but because you make them feel normal.

Now, before they get bored with you, excuse yourself from the conversation. But before you leave, write your name down on a matchbook and as you hand it to them say, "Give me a call next time you're in town. We'll hang."

Guaranteed, you will be the first person who has given Angela or Bill a matchbook with a name and number and invited them to "hang" in over twenty years. Obviously, the chances of their responding to this simple and unpretentious invitation and calling you are slim to none. But because by now you are a great social climber, odds are you'll run into them again at another big party where they will undoubtedly be surrounded by even more obvious climbers. Which means there is a better than fifty-fifty chance that they will use you and your story of your imaginary cheetah bite to escape yet another boring conversation, i.e., the Unicorn will actually say hello to you. You have now begun to flip the power dynamic.

If you're lucky, a photographer will take your picture with the Unicorn, and when that appears in a magazine or on a blog, you will now be officially friends with a Unicorn. Female readers who were discreet enough not to have mentioned to the press that, when they first showed their wounded thigh to Bill

Clinton, he offered to change their bandage in the back of his limousine will now also be officially trustworthy to both Bill and Hillary, giving them yet another reason to call you when they are in town.

Of course, if you pull off the above, you will either have to wear pants whenever you next see Bill/Angelina or self-mutilate a wound worthy of a baby cheetah. But there is no arguing that is a small price to pay for the entrée to be gained by being new best friends with a Unicorn.

Note: We are not being facetious about the cheetah bite ploy. In our research we came across an ex-supermodel who charmed the New York social set with tales of a tropical childhood that she would illustrate by revealing a jagged scar just above her bikini line, which she would heroically explain was the result of a childhood shark bite. Men felt particularly sorry for her when she detailed the number of lingerie jobs she lost to the unsightly wound, and in a few short years, her scar helped her hobnob her way to a marriage with an Italian industrialist with a textile empire. It was only later, when we tried to locate the account of the shark bite in her hometown newspaper, that we discovered the scar was in fact the result of an infected boil.

But to fully understand the benefits of tricking a Unicorn into thinking you've been bitten by a wild animal, let's backtrack for a moment to the World Wildlife Fund charity event at which you first encountered the Unicorn. When you return to the table of the Big Fish who invited you, he or she will have observed you talking to Bill or Angelina. Because of this, he or she will not be annoyed you've stayed away from the table for an unacceptable length of time. Instead, he or she will be overjoyed and inquire, "Why didn't you tell me you were friends with Bill/Angelina?"

To which you will answer, "You never asked me."

When your Big Fish host wants to know the details of your conversation, do not push your luck with the cheetah bite story, simply say, "Just gabbing with old friends." Which in the alternate universe the social climber lives in, they are.

As a "friend" of Bill Clinton or Angelina Jolie, your value to the Big Fish who invited you to the charity gala has been exponentially raised to the tenth power. In short, the game has been changed.

Because of your newfound status, you will be invited to twice as many galas and parties as before, thus increasing the likelihood that you'll bump into your Unicorns again into an inevitability. They won't remember your name or your face, but they will recall your wound. If you have been doing your homework and, say, discovered from reading the tabloids while waiting in line at the supermarket that your Unicorn has a ten-year-old daughter, ask them how she's doing in math. Because Unicorns talk to too many people to remember what they say to anyone, they will assume that in a previous encounter, they must have confided in you. Because most people whom they encounter at galas are either embarrassingly flattering or trying to get them to attend yet another fund-raiser party, they will be relieved to have run into someone real enough to talk about what is real to them, i.e., their daughter's inability to master long division.

A Whale, seeing you talking earnestly with a Unicorn about their daughter, will assume that someone so comfortable with one Unicorn must know many Unicorns, and will invite you to the next dinner they are throwing for Prince William or George Soros, and most game-changing of all for you, when you meet Prince William or George Soros, you'll be introduced as the old friend of Bill Clinton or Angelina Jolie.

No Unicorn wants to be the first Unicorn friend of a non-Unicorn. But now that you're Angelina's or Bill's pal, it will be safe for them to become your new best friend.

The rules of Unicorn friendship are as follows:

1. If a Unicorn asks you to do anything with them, you must always say yes even if you have a surgical procedure scheduled for that day.

2. When a Unicorn calls you on the phone, you must be willing to talk as long as they want to talk about anything, most especially about themselves and the unfair burdens of fame.

3. Never, never, never talk to the press, unless instructed by the Unicorn to disseminate their side of a story, i.e., be prepared to lie on spec.

4. The Unicorn is always right, especially when they contradict themselves.

5. If they contradict themselves in public, merely point out that their statement reflects the paradoxical nature of the universe, as opposed to confirming their rumored alcohol or drug dependency.

6. Though it is easier to become new best friends with Unicorns who do drugs and/or drink to excess, they will

inevitably blame you for their addiction. Better to use alcohol/drugs to cement the relationship, and then suggest that you both take a few weeks off and go to a rehab facility with five-star spa service together.

Unicorns are hard work; being friends with one is a full-time job. Though they will buy you costly presents, pick up the checks for obscenely expensive meals, send their limos to collect you, and treat you to lavish holidays in Unicorn watering holes, it's important you periodically say no to the freebies their other social climbing friends are accepting. Never say no to spending time with them or to a freebie Unicorn holiday, but occasionally say no when the limo is offered, and insist on paying for your own taxi. Once a year, pass on the ride in the private jet and fly on your own dime. Doing this accomplishes two things: a) It separates you from their other freeloading friends, and b) since normal people pay their own way, by doing so on occasion, you maintain the illusion that you are normal, which then gives Unicorns the illusion that they are normal because they are friends with a normal person as opposed to a total freeloader. Remember, no matter how generous Unicorns may seem, they are always paranoid that they are being used by social climbers.

Never try to repay the generosity of a celebrity with Unicorn status by inviting them to your home. Though famous people will be amused to hear anecdotes about the little headaches of your normal life—your toilet that requires a plunger to flush fully or the family of mice that lives in your oven—they will not be amused by firsthand encounters with your faulty toilet or rodent problem.

EMPOWERING THOUGHT #40

The key to maintaining a long-term friendship with a Unicorn is to identify a specific need that the Unicorn keeps hidden from the rest of the world, the most common being the Unicorn's desire for unconditional love.

If your Unicorn asks you if you think so-and-so is taking advantage of their generosity, i.e., using them, do not answer directly. A definitive yes or no will risk making an enemy of a rival social climber. Better to respond with a question that will expose the nature of their closeted neediness, such as, "Do you feel used?" which will open the door for them to inadvertently reveal how much they spend a year buying friends. This is an important figure for you to remember—ask yourself, are you being appropriately compensated for all the hours you've spent listening to them complain about how hard it is to be famous? Then volunteer, "I just think someone in your position has to be very careful to avoid becoming friends with takers, as opposed to givers." You have now subliminally identified yourself as a giver.

To deepen your budding friendship with your Unicorns, you must separate them from as many of their old friends as possible. If, for example, your Unicorn is a movie star, and his or her friends suggest that he or she is too thin, and you hear them encouraging the Unicorn to put on a few pounds, in private suggest that those seemingly concerned about the Unicorn being underweight have selfish reasons for wanting the Unicorn to get fat.

Unicorns need to hear what they want to hear. It is your job to cater to that need before they ask one of their other new best friends if they think you are taking advantage of them. In short, think of the Unicorn as Stalin and yourself as the head of the secret police, Beria.

Set yourself apart as a new best friend above suspicion. If you and the rest of your Unicorn's entourage have been invited to a five-star event—say, Graydon Carter's Oscar party—pull your Unicorn aside just before you get out of the limo and surprise them by suggesting that you both do something more meaningful than hitting yet another red carpet and invite them to do something really special: bowling. Unicorns trust bowlers; nothing is more normal than bowling. Being a Unicorn, they won't ditch the party, but because it has been so long since they have been bowling and because no one but you would exchange an opportunity to be seen at the Oscar party to bowl, you will have set yourself apart as the kind of normal person the Unicorn's shrink has urged them to establish friendships with and you still get to go to the party.

Like Unicorns, certain types of Whales can change your life overnight. By our definition, a Whale is a Big Fish with over $100 million. Note: Whales in this category like to be referred to as centimillionaires rather than simply multimillionaires. However, billionaires, even if they have multiple billions, are confident enough to be comfortable with simply being referred to as billionaires. Some Unicorns—Paul McCartney, Oprah, Ivanka Trump, et al.—are also Whales, but not all Whales are Unicorns, i.e., a Unicorn cannot walk down the street without being recognized, while many Whales can, unless they have hired a good publicist. On the other hand, there are Whales, such as Shorty Guzmán (according to *Forbes*, the forty-first most-powerful person in the world and the reputed head of the Sinaloa drug cartel), who pay people to *keep* them from being recognized on the street. (Mr. Guzmán's recent arrest only proves that if a Whale has accumulated enough money to become a Unicorn, he will be recognized whether he likes it or not.) Such is the voodoo of money.

For the truly ambitious Mountaineer, the magical power of a Unicorn to transport the climber to the top of the mountain is exceeded only by that of the most endangered species of game changer, the Whale family.

Whale families are pods of multigenerational wealth, by-products of a family fortune usually founded by a Whale more than a hundred years ago, whose descendants, due to luck, temperance, strategic marriages, shrewd investments, Prohibition, manipulation of tax loopholes, and an uncanny ability to make money off both sides in any and every war, have grown richer with each subsequent generation. Often, but not always, Whale families have a last name that appears on a product used by millions of people every day.

In general, wealth counselors agree that the financial rule of thumb as regards most American family fortunes is bootstraps to bootstraps in three generations. But Whale families are the exception. Individually, the members of the pod may only be worth $100 million each, but families in which there are thirty-five centimillionaire cousins, two billionaire parents, and four multi-billionaire grandparents are a force to be reckoned with. It isn't simply the collective net worth in dollars that makes Whale families so popular with social climbers. It is the collective clout of the social and political power, connections, influence, etc., they have accumulated over the last hundred years, coupled with their billions, that makes them irresistible to the ambitious Mountaineer.

> In our opinion, anyone who has had a billion-plus for more than six months qualifies as old money.

The flash appeal of such fortunes will be covered in our Advanced Mountaineering chapter. However, in terms of game changers, it is worth noting at this point that hanging out with a single Russian billionaire, such as Roman Abramovich, or Señor Guzmán, or hedge fund billionaire Steve Cohen might have its charms, but it does not have the same panache as hobnobbing with the Rockefellers, the Kennedys, the Rothschilds, the DuPonts, or the Fords who make the car.

These pods of family wealth and social cachet have always had a special allure to Mountaineers. But before attempting to ascend the cliff face of such a clan, you should know that they are as difficult and frosty a climb as Everest. Why? Because they've had more than a hundred years' experience dealing with social climbers, and they are families, and all families are complicated.

The perks that make friendship with a Whale family so enticing are obvious—the family compounds, vast estates, private beaches, guesthouses that go empty for months at a time, private planes, yachts, personal chefs waiting to make you a tuna melt in the middle of the night. The Whale family's appeal isn't simply that they belong to the best clubs or throw the most lavish parties, it's that they have spent the last century accumulating juice in every walk of life. They haven't just elected presidents and built gymnasiums, hospitals, and libraries at all the right schools, they have made all the right friends and have banked a century's worth of favors.

A phone call from the elder of a Whale family can take you anywhere you want to go, but unfortunately, few climbers ever make it past the front gate of the family compound.

To begin with, most Mountaineers make the mistake of being overconfident. Why? Because the chances are that the Whale in the pod that you've met, believe to be your NBF, and think you can use to advance yourself is invariably the prodigal, the black sheep, the runt, the heir or heiress going through their Big City party girl/boy phase or their do-gooder phase and/or are more likely than not, three weeks away from entering rehab. The fact that you have become friends with the most embarrassing member of the pod will make the family suspicious of you before they've even met you. They may smile and say, "Pleased to meet you," but what they're thinking is, "Ye gads, what has the cat dragged in this time?"

Regardless of whether the Whale family member you've had the good fortune to meet is the pod's wastrel or the golden boy/girl of the clan, it is important for you to realize that you are playing the long game. The smart social climber recognizes from day one that the long-term value of this connection will not come if you simply charm and ingratiate yourself with a single member of an old-money family. That works with Unicorns, but not Whales with bloodlines. The real benefits in terms of accessing the entrée and networking connections the pod has built up over generations will come only if you charm and ingratiate yourself with the whole pod.

> Though the members of an immensely rich multigenerational-wealth family, aka a Whale family, may say scathing things about their own family's indolence, untrustworthiness, cruelty, wastefulness, or lack of social conscience when talking to you (someone who isn't a member of the one percent), what they aren't saying is that though they don't trust their family, they trust you and the rest of the 99 percent even less.

Given that every Whale family has had unfortunate experiences with blackmail, kidnapping, lawsuits from injured houseguests, and countless messy and expensive divorces, not to mention exploitation by short-sighted social climbers, this mistrust is not entirely unjustified.

Families who have inherited vast amounts of money are often genuinely curious about people like yourself. They want to know what it's like to actually have to go to an office because you will be fired if you don't, as opposed to having an office to go to so you don't have to spend all day shopping, playing golf, and doing Pilates and yoga.

Because these families have been around for so long, they know who is who and who *was* who, i.e., if you have invented an imaginary great-aunt with a villa in Cap d'Antibes to impress the chain of Big Fish that led you to meet a member of a Whale family, do not mention her in front of the rest of the clan.

Because you are a novelty, and members of Whale families are inherently and innately mistrustful of those who do not come from Whale families, the member of the Whale family you've befriended will be curious to see what the rest of his/her pod thinks of you. Politely but firmly refuse any and all invitations to meet other members of the pod one or two at a time. No matter how good an impression you make, they will go back to the family compound and say bad things about you to the rest of the pod. Whale families keep their teeth sharp by undercutting family members who aren't present to defend themselves or their social climbing new best friends, i.e., you.

With a Whale family, it is an all-or-nothing proposition. You need the whole family to love you, not just one or two. Note:

If you are one of our readers who is considering sleeping your way to the top, do not have sex with the first member of the multigenerational member of the family you meet. Why? Because if you follow our advice, you will have the pick of the pod. Remember, in Whale families, not all trust funds are created equal.

Equally important, when getting to know the Whale family member you hope will introduce you to his/her pod, it is best to show no interest in discussing or meeting his/her esteemed family. The more unimpressed you seem, the more the solitary Whale who is adrift in the real world will reveal about the other members of his/her pod. Because your ultimate goal is to seduce the entire pod, this information will be of vital importance.

What you read on the Internet or glean from the research sources that have been so invaluable in getting the lowdown on Big Fish will already have been heavily edited by the pod's lawyers and PR firms and be of little or no value. A drug bust and time spent in a Turkish jail will appear in Wikipedia as a cross-cultural philanthropic field trip. The good news for the climber is that Whale family members who have been temporarily banished from the pod for bad behavior or are on sabbatical in a funky part of the Big City to gain "life experience" will be homesick and therefore indiscreet. If you pretend *not* to be interested in talking about the pod, they will tell you all of their Whale family secrets.

Why are lonely Whales so indiscreet?

a) They know everybody likes to hear sordid details about Whale family life.

b) Trashing their relatives for being greedy, decadent, and abusive of power is a polite way of bragging.

c) They want to be the center of attention and do all of the talking.

d) They will want to make sure you won't believe all the bad/embarrassing things the other pod members will tell you about them.

Given that they were born Whales and have more disposable income than they can spend and more entrée than they can use, what do born Whales have to complain about? Basically, in Whale families the angst boils down to: Who was Grandpa or Grandma's favorite, i.e., who got the most money or voting shares of stock or the all-important seat on the family's foundation? Whereas a normal family would argue about who took recently deceased Uncle Billy's Jumbotron TV while the rest of the clan was at the funeral home, Whales have art collections, heirloom jewelry, attics full of priceless antique furniture, yachts, private jets, etc., to borrow but not return. Infighting and backbiting among the pod is exacerbated by staggeringly high stakes and the complexity of tax laws governing the distribution of multigenerational wealth.

EMPOWERING THOUGHT #41

No member of an über-rich Whale family is ever certain about his or her position in the pod due to the fact that, in spite of the number of toys and assets the family may have, not everyone can play with all the toys at once. Lawyers are ever ready to alter and update wills. Love cannot be parceled out as equitably as money, but the going exchange rate is understood by all, and more important, should be understood by you, the social climber, before taking on the whole pod.

Because you don't know any of the other pod members yet, the Whale family scion you have befriended will be more forthcoming about his/her relatives than he/she would be if he were speaking to a fellow Whale. As with the Unicorn, you will suffer through long and boring monologues about the hardships and heartaches that go hand in hand with having been born with having so much. Take notes: This is recon time. When you finally do wangle an invitation to spend the night with the extended Whale family at their compound, it will be important for you to know whether it was their cousin Bobo or Coco whose aversion to the color purple caused her to set fire to the guest room containing an unlucky Mountaineer who made the mistake of wearing a lavender dress.

Once you have acquired a clear understanding of the family dynamics at work, grudges, pet hates, prejudices, intergenerational feuds, and rarefied interests of the whole clan, you will have a tactical edge. But to make the most of that advantage, it is essential that you do not accept an invitation to accompany the Whale back to his/her family's watering hole unless you are absolutely sure the whole pod will be present.

Members of a Whale family, like all humans, are innately aggressive and competitive. However, due to their obvious advantages—money, connections, and power that come with their last name—and disadvantages, such as emotional damage done by governesses with harsh toilet-training techniques, lack of love, and learning disabilities due to inbreeding, playing games with outsiders is not fun for Whales. They prefer to release their aggression by being viciously competitive with the other members of the pod, all of whom they have good reasons not to trust, due to the simple fact that wills can always be changed. In other words, the Whale family will compete for what you can offer, and they are clearly in short supply of— human warmth.

If the Whale family contains, say, twenty-five members, it will be obviously impossible for you to charm and ingratiate yourself with every member of the pod simultaneously. However, if you get your Whale to invite you for a "family weekend," the clever and disciplined climber can give every single member of the pod the illusion that you like him or her best.

> Even if you're just a mediocre guest, an average dispenser of compliments and maker of polite conversation, Whale families see so few non-Whale outsiders they will still compete for your friendship. Be careful. They will be attracted to you because of your novelty, but you do not want to become a novelty food.

Also know that even in the most benign Whale family, the visiting Mountaineer should be friendly but never too friendly. Ms. Johnson remembers being a guest at a Whale compound when a daughter who had spent the year studying art in Florence returned home with an Italian boyfriend. He was charming, witty, and knew just enough English to sound sincere. When the daughter mentioned the fact that he was an *idràulico*, the Whale family immediately assumed he was a hydraulic engineer. It was only when a toilet became clogged that the Whales realized that *idràulico* is an Italian plumber.

Curiously enough, the Whales weren't put off by the fact that this Italian Mountaineer was a plumber; what they took offense at was that fact that he fixed their clogged toilet not with a plunger but by creating a vacuum with a hand-embroidered face towel.

WARNING

Whales have teeth, even if they are vegetarians, and chowing down on the visiting climber is blood sport for the pod. You are important to them because

> you are a new toy to fight over. The favors and priv-
> ileges the Whale family offers will only keep com-
> ing if you convince each individual family member
> that he or she has a chance of stealing you away
> from the pod member who escorted you in.

Not all the advice we gave you in the Secrets of Being a Great Guest chapter applies to sleepovers with the Whale pod. Whereas Big Fish invite a small fish to their second home and fill your days with activities to make you envy them and their lifestyle, Whale families have so much more of everything, they don't need to be reassured. They already know you envy them, and they assume you, like everyone else, wish you were part of their family. They will feel no obligation and make no special effort to entertain you—they know you are lucky to be in their midst. There will be no need for you to feign being religious or pretend to have to attend your house of worship, head off to cemeteries in search of nonexistent relatives, or retreat to your room to pray to Mecca to gain time for yourself. You can count on the fact that you will be ignored for long stretches of the day.

The trick for you, the climber/houseguest, is to engage the family in a way that does not make it seem as if you are pursuing them. Whales do not feel obliged to entertain their guests. Do not be surprised if the pod member who brought you home immediately deserts you and retreats to their childhood bedroom to see if anyone has taken any of their old toys. To avoid being mistaken for a prowler we recommend that immediately upon arrival you announce that you are tired and ask to be shown to your room so you can take a nap. Whales don't feel guilty about sleeping during the day.

When all the family members are present downstairs, join them . . . carefully. Do not make a grand entrance. Slip into the room as though you had come to steal the silver and look for an imperious woman over the age of seventy whose coiffure indicates someone has been paid to wash her hair every day for over a half century. Why? Because nearly all Whale pods are ruled by a matriarch. If the Whale who has invited you has not identified her by name and/or physical characteristics, she will invariably be the one who has the most dogs around her.

> Before introducing yourself to the Whale matriarch, or any other members of the family, make a point of introducing yourself to their dogs. Their pets' opinion of houseguests carries great weight in Whale families.

If you don't like dogs, get over it. How do you introduce yourself to a dog? Just the way you would to anyone else you wanted to like you. Say, "Hello, good boy!" . . . "Aren't you the smartest dog in the world?!" Rub their stomach and don't wipe your fingers if they slobber on your hand.

EMPOWERING THOUGHT #42
The matriarch of a Whale Family is more likely
to judge you by her dogs' reaction to you than

by her children's or any other relative's opinion of you, for the simple reason that Whale matriarchs are far fonder of their pets than they are of their own blood relations.

If the matriarch has, for example, corgis, when she introduces herself the first words out of your mouth should not be, "Hello," or "Pleased to meet you," but "I grew up with corgis." Bond over corgi love. Tell the boss lady Whale the names of each of the corgis you never had, and make up a sad story about how heartbroken you were when one of them died. Be careful not to say your imaginary dog died of distemper or was run over by a car. Dog-loving Whales will blame you for letting them run off the leash, or for not taking them to the vet when they were sick. Instead, tell the matriarch your Corgi died happily chasing rabbits in its sleep at the age of eighteen—126 in dog years, which is almost as long as the matriarch expects to live.

Now if the member of the pod who brought you for the weekend knows that you are not a dog lover and interjects, "You told me you're a cat person," smile and say, "You're just saying that so your mother/grandmother/great-aunt won't like me." Though this might sound childish, old-money Whales are childish, and most important, you have now set the stage for the competition for your friendship.

After winning over the matriarch by allowing her dogs to hump your leg, the order in which you befriend the other members of the pod does not particularly matter. Because you have a great many Whales to charm and a limited amount of time to do it in, do not waste time ingratiating yourself with members of the family whose opinion does not matter to the rest of the pod, i.e., don't waste words with those who have married into the pod, unless of course they are the family's financial advisor, attorney, psychic advisor, or they themselves are members of a separate Whale family. This is where your recon research will come in handy.

In each of your subsequent conversations, with the right siblings, cousins, and extended family members, they will inevitably try to trick you into saying something negative about the member of the pod who has brought you. If the family member who brought you has a stutter, an obvious weakness—say, a history of drug abuse—or is out on bail for a felony, do not get duped into giving your opinion of his or her past misbehavior, culpability, or weaknesses. Simply say the truth: "It must be hard, being a Rockefeller/Kennedy/Rothschild"; if pushed to explain what you mean, know they will find you irresistible if you say, "The world holds you to a higher standard than it does the rest of us." Also know that if you say this they will take advantage of this opportunity to tell you why being a member of their Whale family was harder for them than it was for any of the other members of the pod.

Give each member of the pod thirty minutes of one-on-one in the pity pot, and don't forget to include the corgis in all conversations. If the Whale who brought you complains that you are not spending enough time with him or her, explain that you are just being polite. Do not under any circumstances say anything favorable about your Whale's brothers/cousins/sisters/parents. If pushed to give an opinion on any of the above, simply repeat the phrase you've been uttering all day, "It must be hard being a Rockefeller/Kennedy/Rothschild."

> Obviously, when swimming with a Whale family, there are certain subjects to avoid. Any social climber with a lick of common sense knows that when Mountaineering among the Kennedy family, one should not mention the word "Chappaquiddick." Some verboten subjects are more obscure. The Rockefeller pod, for instance, will not be amused by cannibal jokes, due to the fact that Michael Rockefeller was said to have been eaten by headhunters in New Guinea in 1961.

Remember, Whale families have feelings. And though they will be insensitive to your feelings, you must never be insensitive to theirs. Immense privileges come to those who succeed in seducing the pod. But there are responsibilities. When you travel abroad with the family in their jet to enjoy a private tour of the Louvre, know that when a member of the pod refuses to take your advice to throw away the drugs you told them not to bring in the first place and gets busted in French Customs, you, not the corgi, will be asked to take the blame.

WARNING
If you happen to find yourself a passenger when a Whale family member is in the driver's seat of

a speedboat, car, or plane, and they run over an innocent bystander, you will be asked to tell the police you were driving. Do not believe the Whale family or their attorney when they tell you that if you do take the blame for the delinquent pod member, they will use their collective Whalepower to make sure you get off with probation.

Do not listen to them or their lawyers' promises of eternal gratitude or lifetime employment. Know that once you're in the slammer, the Whale matriarch will tell her dogs, "We never liked that one, did we, poochies?" Worse, years later, when the family member you took the fall for runs for Senate, he or she will reference the incident as a character-defining moment in their lives and say something such as, "It wasn't easy turning my friend in to the police for what they did. But the one thing my family's taught me is that hard decisions are the ones that make us who we are."

If you find yourself a passenger/bystander/witness in such a misadventure, our advice is to make a quick, confidential agreement with the pod's matriarch in which you agree not to talk to the authorities in exchange for a six-figure gift. However, if you are asked by the pod to provide an airtight alibi that can save the heartache and embarrassment that will come to a pod member who is convicted of manslaughter, you should always get a lawyer to help you appraise what your integrity is worth.

EMPOWERING THOUGHT #43

While Whales will always ditch the social climber who is stupid enough to take the blame for a Whale's misadventure with the law, the climber who is smart enough to lie for them in court will become a highly valued, lifelong friend of the whole Whale family.

18 |

MOUNTAINEERING WITH
THE ONE PERCENT

The Zen of social climbing lies in the fact that the climb is never over. True enlightenment comes only when you realize that no matter how high you climb, there is always someone above you looking down their nose at your accomplishments.

In this section of our bible, we will outline the challenges, choices, and rarefied pleasures you will encounter at the high end of the food chain. High-altitude climbing is confusing, even if you're used to the dizzying side effects of fame and fortune. For example, was certified Unicorn and songbird Taylor Swift social climbing when she dated Robert F. Kennedy's grandson Conor Kennedy in Hyannis? Or was young Conor trying to hitch the family wagon to a star?

If you are a Big Fish spending sixty hours a week chained to a desk, compromising friends, family, and personal ethics to build up the kind of war chest it takes to pay for the thrill of swimming with Whales as equals, read this chapter carefully.

How the very rich social climb will be equally invaluable to socially ambitious but financially challenged readers who want to enjoy the perks of Whaledom without having to do the years of boring work and ethical compromises that go into actually becoming a self-made Whale.

Yes, you can have all the fun that comes to those who no longer have to fly commercial, know the joys of yachting, stay in the $50 million beach house, etc., without ever having to suffer for it. But know this: To survive, much less make the most of a weekend spent at the summit of this mountain of excess and enjoy all the toys you deserve to play with but can't afford, you must understand the psychology and etiquette involved in social climbing among self-made Whales.

Why do Whales need to social climb if they're already Whales? The simple answer to that is that not all Whales are created equal.

> Though there is a vast difference in the number and quality of NBFs a Whale can buy depending on whether the Whale is worth $100 million or $10 billion, even the largest Whales have one thing in common with the rest of us—they want what they can't have.

Whales feel they have earned the right to have the best of everything. The trouble is that, given that there are approximately ten thousand people in the world worth more than $100 million and three thousand in America alone, there isn't enough of the very best or even the second best to go around for most

Whales to feel they are getting their fair share of the dream that inspired them to become Whales in the first place.

The demand for the exceptional, the extraordinary, the exquisite, the prime, the ultradeluxe, the rare, and best of all, the "one of a kind" outstrips the supply, hence the Whale is both frustrated and driven by his or her longing for more and the shortage of the very best.

EMPOWERING THOUGHT #44

Whether it's owning Blue Period Picassos or becoming NBFs with ex-presidents of the United States, there are far fewer Whale status symbols than there are Whales who are social climbing to obtain them. Which is bad news for the Whale but good news for the Mountaineer. Market side economics forces Whales to make do palling around with social climbers like yourself.

The Whale's dilemma is further exacerbated by the fact that what qualifies as "the best" is subjective. Is it simply the most expensive or is it the most difficult to obtain? This fundamental quandary permeates and infects every area of a Whale's social life. But it is most gut-wrenching for the Whale who gets to that stage of life when they feel the need to join a club. For the best clubs are often not necessarily the most expensive clubs to join but the most difficult to get into.

For Whales to have the top of the line when it comes to club membership, they not only have to risk semipublic rejection, they also have to do something that a great many Whales in their grandiosity have fooled themselves into thinking life would no longer require of them, i.e., they have to suck up to people who in many cases have less money that they do.

To give Big Fish who think they have the wherewithal to move up a weight class and join a Whale club a practical idea of what is in store for them, and to provide less financially fortunate readers who hope to be their guests a sense of appreciation for what their new Whale friends have had to go through in order for them to invite you to swim or sail, or to play croquet, tennis, or golf at "the" club, consider the following scenario.

Getting into the Club

Suppose you are a freshly minted centimillionaire named Chester. You have made your pile of lucre in the heartland— say, Phoenix, Tallahassee, Spokane, or Scranton. Most important, you, Chester, absolutely love to play golf. It's more than a game, it's an eighteen-hole religion. The dream that has sustained you while you slaved for your millions was that one day you would be able to play golf whenever you wanted on the manicured greens of one of America's fabled East Coast old-money WASP country clubs.

Perhaps the club of this ilk that you prefer is East Hampton's Maidstone Club. Founded in 1887, it features eighteen holes that border the priciest stretch of beachfront in the all the Hamptons, grass tennis courts by the dozen, a mock Tudor clubhouse that overlooks an Olympian pool, cabanas, beach club, and private surfside bathing beach. Maybe your dream club is Oyster Bay's Piping Rock, which features a pillared white colonial clubhouse, grass tennis courts, clay tennis courts, indoor tennis courts, and, of course, a golf course that looks out at the very same stretch of Long Island Sound that inspired Gatsby's dream.

Or perhaps your fancy is Pennsylvania's famed Rolling Rock—the club, not the beer—where two-thousand-acre grounds allow you to shoot game birds and foxhunt in addition to playing tennis and golf. Or, if you're a West Coast Whale, there is San Francisco's Olympic Club, which, besides being the oldest athletic club in America, offers not just one but three golf courses and a lakeside clubhouse and a city clubhouse where you can play squash. Whatever . . . for the purpose of this exercise, let's say Chester's golf dream is an old-money WASP club called Lord's Point.

Under the above circumstances, what are Chester's chances of getting into the fictional Lord's Point, or the very real Maidstone, Piping Rock, Rolling Rock, or any of the other old-money WASP clubs all golf-playing Whales want to belong to? ZERO.

How can that be, you ask? Chester has all of his fingers and toes, he knows how to say please and thank you, not to make cellphone calls in club facilities, and is a master of polite conversation. And besides having a BA and an MBA, he's a scratch golfer.

While having a hundred million makes Chester a bona fide Whale in Spokane or Tallahassee or Scranton, that alone will not get Chester real or metaphorical membership in any of the Whale clubs in the vicinity of New York, Los Angeles, Palm Beach, etc. Even if Chester's business acumen is such that since he began reading this chapter, he managed to turn his centimillion into a billion, Chester would still have some serious social climbing to do before he will be in a position to even apply.

Why? Because the game those who already belong to WASP country clubs enjoy even more than golf is making wannabe members suffer the same indignities that they had to go through to gain admission. Especially if the wannabe has more money than they do.

What should Chester do? To begin with, Chester, like every reader of *The Social Climber's Bible*, even those with money to burn, should look at himself in the mirror and take stock of his nonbankable assets. Unfortunately, looks and charm do not go far at WASP clubs.

Top-tier Whale clubs no longer include discriminatory language in their club rulebooks prohibiting memberships on the basis of race, religion, or sex, except for the exclusive Pine Valley Golf Club in New Jersey that not only doesn't allow women to be members but is open-minded enough to permit the wives of members to play on Sunday afternoons.

Chester should also know that if he happens to be Jewish, he would be in a distinct and very small minority at a WASP club like Lord's Point. Yes, the old days of blatant anti-Semitic membership stipulations are fortunately behind us. But it is curious to note that even today, in most cases, Jewish members of WASP clubs have shiksa wives. As to Muslim membership in WASP clubs, the latest statistics have not yet been compiled. But it is safe to say that Allah will not help you get into the club.

Just for the record, we are adamantly against Chester or anyone else changing their religion, race, or sex to get into a golf club; however, ultimately, that decision is between you and your maker.

Having looked in the mirror, regardless of what he sees, Chester should know before he sets out on his membership quest that he will need to look and act like a WASP even if he isn't one.

> How does a WASP look and act? Just imagine you are suffering from constipation 24/7/365, avoid public displays of affection, never smile at strangers, and never fail to remind the outsider that he or she doesn't belong.

To make the kinds of friends Chester needs to get into the club, he must prove that he is what in club land is often expressed as "committed to the community." Merely renting a house for 50K to 100K a month in one of the Hamptons, Palm Beach, or Hobe Sound will not cut it.

If Chester were trying to get into East Hampton's Maidstone Club, let's say, and had turned his hundred million into a billion, he might be tempted to demonstrate his commitment to "the community" by purchasing a Further Lane manse like the one hedge fund king Steven Cohen recently bought up the beach from Maidstone for $60 million. The trouble is, if he did that, he would be accused of showing off.

Chester, being only a centimillionaire, can't afford to make so risky a splash. But he should be able to demonstrate an acceptable degree of commitment to the community by purchasing an unostentatious shingled cottage close to the golf course for something in the neighborhood of $10 million. Now, if Chester is lucky, after four or five years of spending his summers next to a golf club he can afford to join but doesn't dare mention his desire to join for fear of being rejected on the grounds he's "pushy," Chester might finally be good enough friends with a member to bring up the subject of applying for membership himself.

As with all levels of social climbing, there are of course shortcuts that can be taken to get into Lord's Point or any of the other clubs mentioned. Old-money WASP clubs all pride themselves on being "family clubs," i.e., it is easier to get in if you have a wife and children. Why? Because the little ones' snack bar bills and daily charges at the pro shops and junior camp fees add another zero to a member's annual dues.

Now if Chester already has his wife and spawn, there is no way he is going to be able to get out of having to spend those five years sucking up to club members and pretending to be a WASP. But if Chester is single, or loves the game of golf enough to divorce his wife and ditch his children before he buys into the community, he can cut the membership line by calling in an assist from Cupid and marrying the daughter of a club member as soon as he gets to town. Social climbers have married for less honorable reasons than golf.

Of course, if Chester doesn't want to go that route, there is one way to speed the process of acceptance—he should stop wasting his winters back in Phoenix, Scranton, Spokane, or wherever the hell it was he made his pile and move to where the majority of Whales who belong to his club of choice live the other eight months of the year, i.e., New York, especially the Upper East Side of New York. More specifically, north of Sixty-Third Street and south of Eighty-Fifth, preferably on Fifth or Park Avenues.

A Whale-worthy apartment in a co-op building where the club members reside that he needs to spend more time with will cost in the neighborhood of $20 million. Now Chester has to only read our chapter on social climbing as a family and get his kids into one of the right schools so they can do their part to help him fulfill his dream of teeing off as a member of the club. To cement the strategic friendships he *and* his children are working on once Chester has gotten them into the right schools, it's time for him to show club members his heart as well as his checkbook are in the right place by supporting the right charities.

Chester should know that purchasing a half dozen $1,000 to $2,500 tickets to his NBF's charity events over the course of the year won't cut it. A Whale who wants to get into the kind of club Chester wants to get into before he is too old to play golf will be expected to buy at least one table at charity events such as the Sloane-Kettering Spring Ball, the Robin Hood Foundation gala, the Rainforest Fund party, the Metropolitan Opera opening night, etc. What will that cost Chester? The top table at the cheapest of these events is fifty thousand dollars. The premier table at the most expensive—$250,000.

What would Chester be getting for his money? Well, if his benefit of choice were Robert F. Kennedy Jr.'s Fishermen's Ball, the most environmental and most casual ("blue jeans preferred") of New York City charity galas, purchasing a 100K "Enforcer Table" would be sure to make a more favorable impression on the head of the membership committee than less impressive and costly tables, whose descriptions make one think of cuts of meat—the 50K "Prime Table" or the 25K "Select Table." Though the shabby $12,500 table is described as the "Great Table," it is clearly also the worst table, particularly if Chester is trying to impress other Whales with his largesse.

By now, Chester and his family will have realized that in addition to golf, they will have to master other sports as well. If he or his family admits they didn't grow up playing the "right" sports, they will draw attention to the fact that they are not as "right" as they appeared to be when they bought the Enforcer Table.

EMPOWERING THOUGHT #45

The upwardly mobile Whale can reduce the risk of being labeled NOKD (Not Our Kind Dearie) by mastering all WASP sports in secret; only after two to three years of private lessons in tennis, squash, paddle, skiing, and sailing, should you consider attempting to play with a club member, and when you do so, remember to lie and say that you have not played since you were a child.

Having done all of the above, Chester will be relieved to know he is finally in a position to apply for membership. Unfortunately, part of the application process is being interviewed by the membership committee.

When interviewing to get into an old-money WASP country club, here are some tips that will increase the odds of your making the right impression:

1. Avoid using big words. Why? WASP Whales will not appreciate having you explain that effeminate does not mean the same thing as ephemeral, especially in regard to rumors that you or your son is gay.

2. Even though our social climber's mantra tells you to refuse to be judged, know that you are being judged.

3. Do not wear new shoes. WASPs are suspicious of people who wear new shoes and will assume you bought them because you didn't own appropriate footwear before the scheduling of your interview.

4. Have your wife wear enough jewelry to show you can afford to buy her jewels, but not so much bling as to make your interviewer think that if he lets you into the club his own wife will make him buy her the same expensive jewelry your wife has.

5. Do not mention the fact that you own a yacht, a Ferrari, or a house in Aspen or went to one of the right schools unless you are absolutely certain your interviewer possesses similar or commensurate status symbols—Whales do not like to be made to feel small.

Unfortunately, even if Chester gets through these interviews with flying colors, he will still not be a member of the club. How can that be?

Clubs are not democracies. Part of the fun of the admission rules at WASP golf clubs is that any member who belongs to the club can, if he or she chooses, take exception to Chester or any member of his family's worthiness at the last minute and blackball him.

What are people blackballed for? Any and everything. It is rumored that billionaire heir to a Colombian beer fortune, Alejandro Santo Domingo, and his glamorous *Vogue* editor wife, Lauren, were recently blackballed from the ultraexclusive South-ampton Bathing Corporation, aka the Beach Club. As one anonymous anti–Santo Domingo member of the Beach Club said about Lauren Santo Domingo, "She courts publicity and that is entirely what this club eschews." Which seems to translate as Mrs. Santo Domingo's only sin was being younger, more stylish, and more attractive than other female club members.

Given that Chester has done everything right, there is no need for him to worry about getting blackballed. Right? Wrong. Chester has committed the most unforgivable of sins in the WASP world of clubs—trying too hard.

EMPOWERING THOUGHT #46

If you are rejected by the club of your choice, you should be ashamed—but you should also know that there is a key detail of clubdom that

> is swept under the carpet: Those members who serve on the membership committee are invariably the members who were initially denied club membership and were only accepted after years of sucking up.

The real price of membership to an old-money WASP club is not the $150,000 to $200,000 initiation fee, nor the $50K annual charges that a family of four is likely to incur if they take tennis and golf lessons and frequent the snack bar; it is the cost of all the status symbols they have to acquire in order to be deemed worthy—the $10 million summer house, the $20 million co-op, the millions spent on the right schools, the right vacations, the right charitable donations, etc., plus the time spent making the right friends when one could have been out making more money. Of course, for Whales like Chester, all the expenditure and humiliation involved in becoming a member are well worth it because they allow him to maintain the delusion that he didn't buy his way into "the Club."

Clubs That Aren't "Clubs" but Really Are Clubs

Luckily for Whales and those who enjoy riding the largesse of their wake, there are forms of advanced social climbing that don't involve golf or membership in an old-money WASP club.

If you're a Whale who, like most Whales, already has his own pool, tennis courts, beach, and all the other accoutrements of country club life at your exclusive disposal in your own backyard, or having been accepted into the golf club, have lost interest in golf, there is one club you can join that offers more rarefied, elitist, and cultured fun than the most exclusive country club in the world. Though totally lacking outdoor amenities, it does boast clubhouses in every major city in the world and holds jamborees in an international network of vast palatial edifices where club members are feted and celebrated on a weekly basis somewhere on the globe.

Better yet, at this club's functions nouveau Whales not only get to bond with the most sophisticated and worldly Whales in the world, they get to hobnob with movie stars, supermodels, famous directors, highbrow cultural icons, celebrities from every walk of life, and the latest certified genius of the month. What's more, this club doesn't discriminate on the basis of race, religion, or sexual orientation. In fact, if you're kinky, you'll be doubly welcome.

The best part is, there's no membership fee, no annual dues, no formal application process, no risk of rejection, and no one can blackball you.

We call it the Art Club. And its only membership requirements are that you love to shop and have several hundred million dollars to spend on museum-quality art. Its clubhouses are ultratasteful private galleries with names like Gagosian, Pace, Matthew Marks, Acquavella, White Cube, and Ace, and the palatial settings for your jamborees are the greatest museums in the world.

Besides all the parties, openings, cocktail parties, and celebrity friends that come with the mega spending that is a prerequisite to membership, what makes the Art Club doubly appealing to Whales is, even if you're colorblind, if you buy enough art at the galleries mentioned above, odds are you will have made a very shrewd investment. In fact, statistics indicate the Art Club is as profitable as the best hedge funds. According to Dr. Rachel Campbell of the Finance University of Maastricht, since the 1960s, on average, the art market has gone up 11 percent a year in value. The art market outperforms everything but insider trading. Look at casino king Steve Wynn. He purchased Picasso's *La Rêve* in 2001 for $60 million and in 2013 sold it to then-reigning hedge fund king Steven Cohen for a cool $155 million. And that's *after* he put his elbow through it showing it off to friends.

Not only does the Art Club membership include Whales of every size and description, it existed before the birth of Jesus Christ. Emperors, tyrants, queens, kings, princes of commerce, robber barons, tycoons—their favorite pastime has always been art collecting. Why? Because it allows them to reinvent themselves, i.e., to social climb. One isn't just buying art, one is buying culture, class, sophistication. It doesn't matter how you made your filthy lucre—arms, exploitation of child labor, strip-mining—spend enough of it on art and your sins will be washed away and you'll be heralded as a Whale of taste and breeding.

Keep spending money and the club will never stop throwing parties for you. Between September and June, art galleries, museums, and auction houses in New York, LA, London, Paris, Hong Kong, Basel, etc., have more openings, shows, cocktail parties, art fairs, dinners, and museum benefits than you will have time to attend. Plus there are the parties that all the other Whales in the club will invite you to to show off their collections and try to hondle you into swapping your Damien Hirst for two of their old Franz Klines.

EMPOWERING THOUGHT #47

If you're a Whale who liked trading baseball cards as a kid, the Art Club is for you. Buy enough "blue chip" art and the simple fact that you purchased a painting will increase its value. Think how good you'll feel knowing that your taste, or lack of it, has shaped the aesthetics of the age you live in.

Contemporary art has become the twenty-first-century equivalent of wampum, those strings of shells American Indians once used as money. Just as wampum was worth what the Indians decided it was worth, so it is with art—particularly modern art; its value is arbitrary and nonintrinsic. The market value of art is determined primarily by the ego of the Whale, i.e., what one Whale is willing to pay to keep another Whale from adding it to his or her collection of "wampum."

Yes, critics, dealers, and museum curators play a role in determining what is deemed "great" art or "bad" art. But when it comes to judging what are the best Hirsts, Princes, Koonses, Hockneys, etc., the greatest paintings or sculptures by those modern masters are those the Whale is willing to pay the most money for. Whales have the last word, not critics. Which is yet another reason that Whales love to burnish their image with art.

As long as nouveau Whales keep joining the Art Club, the already astronomical prices are guaranteed to go up—unless there's a war or a plague or . . . Not to leave the reader with a depressing thought, know that the climbing skills that you are learning in this book will still come in handy even if you have to burn your Basquiat to stay warm.

How does one get started climbing for wampum and becoming a member of the Art Club elite? Is it just a club for sophisticated big-city Wall Street billionaires who minored in art history back in college or grew up in Whale families known for their connoisseurship? Do you have to know someone who already belongs to the club?

The simple answer is no, but to show you how the Art Club works, let's say you're a recently widowed forty-two-year-old housewife from the New Jersey suburbs by the name of Vicki, whose late husband was kind enough to leave you the $500 million he made in the toxic waste disposal business.

You, Vicki, know nothing about the art world except what you've seen in the movies and read in the *New York Post*. But you like pretty things, love to shop, and most important, know there's a more glamorous world waiting for you on the other side of the Hudson that you're curious about. The trouble is, you don't have a clue how someone like yourself would ever gain access to the inner circle of that brand of fabulousness.

Believe it or not, Vicki, your personalized invitation to gallery openings, museum galas, parties, and dinners where you'll be hobnobbing with the bold-faced names and beautiful people pictured on the pages of *Vogue* and *Vanity Fair* is just one phone call away. What's the magic number? It's listed in the phone book. In fact, we'll give it to you: (212) 708-9400.

Now, when the operator answers and says "Museum of Modern Art," ask for the acquisitions department and tell whoever answers the phone that you would like to come by tomorrow and give the museum $5 million.

When they hang up on you, have your lawyer call them back and explain that you, Mrs. Nobody from Nowhere, are indeed serious and have in excess of $500 million to cover the check. Also have your lawyer make it clear that you are not interested in making a donation that goes toward the maintenance of the museum's existing programs, or contributing to the construction of a new wing that will have someone else's name on it, or any of the other boring stuff involved in the running of a museum. You want your $5 million to purchase a single painting by a living artist whom they would like to add to their collection. Guaranteed, twenty-four hours later, you will be treated to lunch in the trustees' dining room of the Museum of Modern Art.

During this lunch, you will add another stipulation to your gift. You get to go with them to the famous artist's studio to help them pick out the painting you're buying for the museum.

They will try to talk you out of this. Have your lawyer prepare a contract that includes your stipulations and place it and a cashier's check for $5 million on the table. The museum representative will tell you this is not how they do business, and that they know best how to spend a patron's money. We guarantee, if you politely tell them that you will take the $5 million to another museum, they will snatch the contract out of your hand, sign it, and take the check.

Congratulations, Vicki: You've just become the newest member of the Art Club! Your membership will become official within forty-eight hours, at which point every single one of the most prestigious art dealers in New York City and beyond will have heard about you, the new Art Whale to surface on the scene.

Why did we tell Vicki to specify her $5 million be used to buy a work of art from a famous living artist? Because a dead painter can't tell everyone what impeccable taste and connoisseurship Vicki has.

Vicki should also know that when she goes to the painter's studio, the curator in charge of this acquisition will try to get all the credit for her deciding to spend her millions on this artist whom Vicki never heard of before she joined the club. To prevent this from happening, as soon as Vicki shakes hands with the artist, she should announce that she has always dreamed of owning one of his/her paintings. "As soon as I got my $500 million, I told myself I have to have one. But you're such a fucking genius, it would be selfish of me to hang your painting on my wall; I should put it in a goddamn museum and share it with the whole frickin' world."

We know, it sounds corny and vulgar, but Art Whales say

things like that all the time to artists. In part because famous artists love flattery backed by cash so much, they will show their appreciation for the intelligence Vicki showed by calling them a "genius" by giving her a small work on paper with a personal inscription. Congratulations, Vicki, you now have an art collection.

The curator will be pissed off at Vicki for stealing all their glory until she asks them to become her personal art consultant. Chances are, they will tell her they are honored but, because of a conflict of interest, they can't. The curator will then recommend someone else for the job who will invariably be his/her husband, wife, boyfriend, or girlfriend. An art consultant is generally paid a flat fee, augmented by what Vicki's dead husband would refer to as kickbacks, or favors, schmears that sometimes but not always involve cash. An art consultant is a paid best friend whose job it is to keep you buying museum-quality art and eventually persuade you to donate it to their girlfriend/boyfriend/friend/husband/wife curator at the museum. Because Vicki has read *The Social Climber's Bible*, she will know they are trying to screw her.

Why do we say that? Because there isn't enough museum-quality art available to those new to the game to keep you spending. The dealers won't sell the best paintings/sculpture to you no matter what your art consultant says because they save the best for Whales who are regular customers.

Now that Vicki is a member of the Art Club, the fun and profit for you will come from figuring out a way of screwing more established members out of paintings, sculptures, etc., that they thought they were in line to buy. This is where art collecting becomes a game.

Though we wouldn't presume to tell you what kind of art to collect, you will have more fun and be invited to better parties (which is two-thirds of the reason anyone joins the Art Club) if you collect the works of hot artists who are young enough to have sexy friends, yet not so young as to be a risky investment, as opposed to collecting dead Old Masters.

Do not just let your art consultant arrange meetings only with his or her favorite dealers. Insist on being introduced to the directors of every single one of the top galleries. Knowing that you have given MoMA $5 million, the dealers will be very nice to you. You should also know, Vicki, that no matter what your consultant and the dealers say, the "best" paintings by whatever artists you have expressed interest in will not be shown to you when you go to the gallery. Why? Because you are new to the game. And it is in the "interest of the dealer," i.e., he will make more money, if he sells the best paintings to more established members of the club, due to the fact that being in the collection of an Art Whale with an established, first-rate collection (one that museums covet) will elevate the sticker price of all the other paintings/sculptures by that artist. How do you get around this, Vicki? By using much the same approach your late husband did when he muscled his way into the toxic waste disposal business.

Do not dress up for these initial meetings. The less chic you are, the more seriously you will be taken in the early stages of your Art Club life. (Do not worry, Vicki, very shortly you will have a great many events to buy couturier clothes for.) Look thoughtfully at the first painting you are shown. No matter how ugly, grotesque, shocking, strange, or beautiful the painting may appear to be, tell the dealer it's "too decorative."

Decorative is the worst thing that can be said about a contemporary work of art. While your art consultant and the dealer are trying to figure out if you actually know what you're saying, announce that you are not interested in "studio sweepings." Then ask to use the restroom.

While they think you're in the bathroom, slip into the rooms of picture racks in the back of the gallery. They will be arranged alphabetically. Once you locate the ones that contain canvases by the painter you're interested in, give a shout out to the art dealer and your art consultant in the same tone of voice your late husband used when dealing with garbage men who tried to skim: "Who the fuck you savin' these for?" Again, do not worry about seeming crass. Part of what makes the art world so fun is that it *is* so blatantly crass.

The dealer will of course tell you that they are on hold or are already sold. If the market value of each canvas is, let's say, five hundred thousand dollars, offer to buy three for a million cash, now or never, and the chances are those paintings will magically become unsold and no longer on hold.

You will now be invited to every party, dinner, and opening that dealer throws for the next year. More important, you have established yourself as a savvy connoisseur. When you go to the next gallery, you will be shown better paintings. And you will only have to spend five hundred thousand dollars in total to become that establishment's new best friend. By the time you drop into the third gallery on your list, museum-quality paintings by the hot artist that your art consultant told you to be interested in will be pulled out without your having to pretend to go to the bathroom so you can sneak back into the racks.

Spend $20 million on living painters/sculptors at an assortment of galleries over the next three months, go to the art auctions at Sotheby's, and bid a record price, say, for a Richard Prince painting of a nurse or a Jeff Koons porcelain of Michael Jackson and his monkey, and dealers and museum directors will be fighting over who gets to throw the first party in your honor. Your days will be filled with studio visits. You will now know the thrill of having certified geniuses suck up to you. And you'll be invited to more celebratory events than you can attend, even if you go out seven nights a week and triple-book. Name any person in the world you've always wanted to meet, and a dealer who has something he wants you to buy will arrange it. Sex, drugs, boys, girls, five-course dinners where all the food is blue. You only have to say what you want and there'll be an art dealer ready, willing, and able to give it to you, Vicki.

Donate another $10 million to the Museum of Modern Art, and you're on the board of the Museum of Modern Art, ergo, you're friends with other board members. Which means that in less than six months, you've gone from being a suburban housewife in Jersey to becoming pals with the likes of Wallis Annenberg, Sid Bass, Leon Black, Clarissa Bronfman, Glenn Dubin, Marie-Josée Kravis, Philip Niarchos, Michael Ovitz, Ronald Perelman, David Rockefeller, and Alice Tisch. What will you talk about with these fancy people you had absolutely nothing in common with until you started shopping for art? Art, of course.

People who would have been horrified by your lack of sophistication, taste, and vulgarity less than a year ago will now be inviting you to fly on their private jets to art fairs—Art Basel in Miami, Art Basel in Hong Kong, Art Basel in Basel. Courtesy cars will whisk you round the fair to make sure you get all your shopping done in time to attend even more lavish parties thrown by luxury brands and fashion houses.

For argument's sake, let's say Vicki spends $200 million of her $500 million on art in her first two years as a member of the Art Club. She will not have blown $200 million, she will have made a $200 million investment that in all likelihood is now worth $250 million. When you buy a yacht, a plane, or a Ferrari and try to sell it two years later, it's a secondhand yacht, plane, or Ferrari. Not so with art. Better yet, Vicki's now $250 million collection, if she so desires, can be traded, transported across international borders, sold for cash, and/or be used for collateral. Since banks are happy to loan money on museum-quality contemporary art—especially if it belongs to a collector who's on the board of the Museum of Modern Art, i.e., has the influence to make sure the market values of her favorite artists don't decrease in value—Vicki can leverage her collection and buy even more expensive paintings. Which will be worth even more in another two years because they've spent that time hanging on Vicki's walls.

What someone like our Vicki chooses to do with her collection when she finally shops till she drops is up to her. It is our hope that she does what a good Whale should do and bequeaths part, or better yet all, of it to a museum so it can be appreciated by small fish and Whales alike. To our way of looking at the world, the Art Club is what social climbing can be at its very best.

EMPOWERING THOUGHT #48

If you are Mountaineer with a highly developed sense of aesthetics, possess a Taste Meister's personality traits, and would like to have access to all the parties and perks that come with membership in the Art Club but lack the financial wherewithal to join, do not give up hope. The art world is a service industry in which merely rich social climbers cater to the needs of obscenely rich social climbers. Convince your NBF Whale to invest in art instead of boring stocks and bonds, and the art world will love you almost as much as they love your Whale, plus you might just get a commission.

Mountaineering on Horseback

Equine sports—show jumping, three-day eventing, dressage fox-hunting, polo, etc.—have always had a special appeal to the advanced social climber. Though it lacks the profit potential that comes with membership in the Art Club, the Horse Club, the tightly knit world of horse love, with its devotion to aristocratic traditions and dress code—velvet hard hats, britches that disappear into glistening knee-high leather boots, and scarlet tailcoats—offers Whales a chance to look like old-fashioned snobs while indulging in an extravagant pastime that allows them to act like snobs.

Whereas art collecting is not a child-friendly sport, big-time horse love offers elitist fun and outdoor competition for the whole family. It's a natural for Whales who've just bought a starter estate but have not yet been accepted by the local gentry. Fill those barns and paddocks up with the right kind of horses, and their pedigrees will make up for what yours lacks.

> If you are a middle-aged Whale who is being given the cold shoulder by the horsey set because your new wife was a pole dancer, corset her in a tweed waistcoat, trick her out in a Bernard Weatherill hacking jacket, put a bowler on her head, mount her on a half-million-dollar Danish Warmblood, and she is no longer an ex exotic dancer, she's a horsewoman.

The horse world looks ultra-WASPy, but it isn't anymore. The few remaining WASPs who can afford an equine hobby are too busy torturing guys like Chester who are trying to get into their golf clubs to have any free time to mount up. Being a member of the Horse Club not only gives Whales of all walks of life the feeling they were "to the manor born," it also allows them to look down their noses at those who actually were born in a manor but had to sell the manor and their horses to pay death taxes.

Some Whales join the Horse Club because they've run out of other pricey pastimes to burn money on. For others, it's the adrenaline rush of galloping recklessly across a meadow, whip in hand, coupled with that old-fashioned "Master of the Universe" thrill that comes when you can dismount and berate a stable boy for not mucking out the stalls. But the vast majority of Whales invest the time and money it takes to join the horse world because their child, usually a daughter—aka the Little Princess—wants a pony of her very own.

Naturally, once Mama and Papa Whale get her the pony, she'll want to enter horse shows where the other little princesses with ponies win long silky blue ribbons and silver stirrup cups with their names engraved on them. Whales, being competitive, will soon realize that in horse shows where the pony is the one doing the jumping, the princess with the best jumper, i.e., the most expensive pony, almost always wins the blue ribbon.

Because Whales love their daughters and want them to win, they then get the riding teacher to find their seven-year-old princess a pony that is right for her, i.e., a four-hundred-thousand-dollar pony that, nine times out of ten, will beat the other Whale princess ponies whose cheapskate parents were willing to invest only three hundred thousand dollars in pony flesh.

Aside from being an ideal vehicle for Whales to teach their children the true value of money, horse shows are a great way to let their princesses know just how much in dollars and cents their parents love them. In the process, Mom and Dad get to meet and compete with other Whale parents with horse-loving princesses such as rock legend Bruce Springsteen, famed *SNL* producer Lorne Michaels, and New York City's billionaire former mayor, Michael Bloomberg. Not bad social climbing, eh?

What really makes the horse show world so appealing to Whales who want to make their daughters happy is that it is less disappointing than teaching them to play a game like golf where buying a princess the most expensive clubs won't necessarily ensure she'll be able to put the ball in the hole, much less win.

Of course, your daughter's horse love will become more costly as she grows up. Because ponies go lame, to keep your daughter in the winner's circle she'll need more than one pony. And by the time she's twelve, a four-hundred-thousand-dollar pony will no longer be able to carry her over the jumps required to get her into the winner's circle, even if she is anorexic. By the time she's seventeen, if you love her enough to keep her winning, she'll need a $5 million herd of horses.

All told, the Whale must foot the bill for the horseflesh to keep princess at the top of her game, the horse farm, the indoor riding ring to keep princess dry when she wants to ride on a rainy day, plus the trainer and the trainer's staff and grooms, the veterinarian bills, the fancy horse van, and a luxury mobile home so princess won't have to use the port-o-johns at the show grounds. And then of course, there's getting all those pricey horses, grooms, trainers, and equipment overseas when your daughter wants to compete in Europe against real princesses.

The real benefits that come from the horse world are the values competitive horse sport instills in the young rider, the sense of fair play and the importance of clean living. Ms. Johnson recalls that she obtained an unforgettable life lesson in the dangers of recreational drug use as a teenager when she discovered her favorite horse's prize-winning ability to jump was in part due to the fact that it was addicted to cocaine.

If you don't have a daughter but want an outdoor activity that involves horses and encourages participants to start drinking before breakfast, foxhunting is for you. Imagine the thrill of riding over hill and dale, leaping over post-and-rail fences, wearing a silk top hat and a scarlet tailcoat, atop a twelve-hundred-pound beast with a brain that tells him tree roots are snakes, all the while shouting "Tally-ho" as you gallop after a pack of forty foxhounds on the heels of a fox.

If you like the sound of all that, except that you don't get a thrill out of witnessing a pack of hounds introduce themselves to a fox, join a foxhunt that's a "drag pack." Though chasing only the scent of a fox is less sporting, it does allow you to enjoy all the pleasures of a blood sport with no blood, other than your own, when you fall off.

For youngish Whales who may not be skilled at riding but want that special brand of camaraderie that comes from being on a team they can be sure of making because they own it, the horse world offers polo. Yes, the word "polo" has lost some its glamour since Ralph Lauren trademarked it, but polo is still synonymous with the kind of devil-may-care elitism that Whales love.

Always popular with masters of the universe, polo was a favorite of Genghis Khan and the British upper class, and it will make you feel like an expert horseman or -woman even when you are not. How can that be? Because the other three riders on your polo team will be paid professionals (often Argentineans) who will keep the ball away from you so your team actually has a chance of winning. The great part is, even if you're losing, you get to ride up and down the field swinging your mallet and looking cool.

To have your own team and compete at high-end tournaments you will need to have at least eighteen ponies costing in excess of thirty-five thousand dollars a head. Of course, if you want to win, you will have to purchase souped-up ponies, which can cost as much as two hundred thousand dollars per pony. Add to that grooms, trainers, vets, estate with polo fields, and paying your professional teammates, the best of whom get as much as $150,000 per tournament, plus bonuses if you don't want invariably good-looking and athletic Argies snogging your wife/girlfriend/daughter/son.

Here again the polo player should expect the added expense of flying his herd of ponies to the UK. Why? Because what's the point of playing polo if you can't have a few chukkas with Prince Harry at the Guards Polo Club?

The horse world is rife with social climbing opportunities for those readers who could not afford to purchase a bridle, much less a horse. Why? Because half the fun for the Whales is having people on hand to watch them and their princess dress up in jodhpurs, boots, etc., and jump fences, ride to the hounds, or gallop up and down polo fields swinging a mallet at a ball their professional teammates don't want them to hit.

EMPOWERING THOUGHT #49

Because normal people find it boring and tedious to watch a sport they cannot afford to participate in, horse-loving Whales need social climbers who are good at pretending they find watching boring horse events fascinating, know when to applaud, and are discreet enough not to point out the suspicious algorithm that connects the price of the show horse with the success of the Whale riding it. Mountaineers who can fake horse love will find themselves the wildly popular houseguests of the well-mounted Whale.

Jet Etiquette

Nothing changes the trajectory and velocity of an aspiring Whale's social climb as much as membership in the private jet club. In fact it could be argued that a Whale isn't officially a Whale until they take the plunge and purchase a sky limo. Readers who've accepted the fact that they will never be able to afford even a bare-bones starter jet like the Lear 21 but still hope to hobnob at high altitude should know that Big Fish charter but

Whales own. The type of jet you get a free ride on will tell you much about where your host can take you literally and figuratively.

Lear today, G6 tomorrow. And next year, a 747. That is, unless you're so busy flying around blowing your fortune on jet fuel that you forget to keep making money.

When you are debating what type of plane to buy consider this scenario: All other things being equal, if you and a neighboring Whale in, say, Saint Tropez have both invited Jack Nicholson, Leonardo DiCaprio, Al Gore, and Taylor Swift to competing Fourth of July clambakes and you offered to fly them to Saint Tropez in your secondhand, $20 million Challenger, but your neighbor has offered to fly them in his brand-new $60 million state-of-the-art Bombardier Global 7000, Jack, Leo, Al, and Taylor will be flying in your neighbor's plane and going to his clambake. Of course, Jack, Leo, Al, and Taylor, being Unicorns and Whales, could afford their own jets but they, just like everybody else when it comes to jets, get a special thrill from a free ride, even if it's taking them somewhere they don't especially want to go. There are levels to all games the various subspecies of Whales like to play.

Whales will tell you that they have a jet because their time is valuable or they hate waiting at check-in lines with little people or can't stand taking their shoes off and risking fungal infection in public airports. What they won't tell you is that the real thrill of private jet ownership comes from all the new friends they acquire as soon as they purchase a private jet.

EMPOWERING THOUGHT #50

Bragging about owning a private jet to people you have no intention of offering a ride to is bad manners. Letting social climbers who are less fortunate than yourself know that you own a private jet so they can start sucking up to you is not bad manners.

Always drop the fact that you no longer fly commercial into the conversation casually. Complain about the defroster in the onboard fridge of your Challenger, or the shower on your Citation—let them know you're a real person who encounters the same household hassles at thirty thousand feet that they do in their studio apartment back on the ground.

Also know that when you make casual reference to your private jet, if there is another high-flying Whale in the vicinity, they will challenge you. "I have a Hawker 800 XP, what kind of bird do you fly?" Now if you also have the Hawker 800 XP, you can have a bonding conversation about the relative merits of their various seat configurations and upholstery options. Which will bore the people who are sucking up to you for a free ride. You, being a Whale, will also know that any competition between Whales that ends in a draw is a loss. Because the whole reason you became a Whale is not just that you always like to be the winner, but that you enjoy the concept of those other than yourself as losers.

How do you top a Whale who has the exact same jet you do without announcing you're trading your Hawker for an Airbus? Simply say, "What I like most about flying is my pilot." Then reveal that your pilot was a combat ace who shot down seven MiGs in Desert Storm, or was the Captain of Air Force One. Even if your rival makes the same claims about their pilot, you will still have won because you thought of lying first.

The social climber who has multiple jet-owning friends never need wait in an immigration line, suffer an unwanted X-ray, or endure the indignity of a body-cavity search again.

Five things to remember about jet etiquette

1. When a Whale with a jet says, "Wheels up at seven a.m.," he or she means you are onboard and the plane takes off at 7:00 a.m. Unless you are a very, very attractive guest, or the Whale with the jet wants something else from you, they will not think it rude, if you are not there on time, to take off without you. Why? Because jet fuel is expensive, it's their plane, they make the rules, and when they arrive, they damn well want to get a swim in before lunch.

2. Always ask what kind of jet you're flying in and how many people will be on board, before you get to the airport. Google the specs on the jet you're riding on. If you're heading to the Caribbean on, say, a Challenger 800, and twelve passengers will be on board, know that one of you is going to have to spend the flight sitting by themselves in the back of the plane on the toilet; this is not where you want to sit. Always

be the first to board the plane and show your host the courtesy of not occupying the two most forward front-facing seats unless you are the host's or hostess's date. Instead, sit directly across from them in the two seats that face backward. If the owner tells you to get up and move to the toilet seat in the back, know that you have some serious sucking up to do.

3. Always bring a present for the owner. Note: A jar of your fruit compote will not cut it as token payment for a seat on a private jet, unless of course the owner has specifically requested it, or you have been told in advance that you are going to be sitting on the Challenger's toilet.

4. Do not admit you have never been on a private jet before. Do not fail to mention how much bigger and nicer your host's jet is than the last private jet you flew in was, even if you are a noncommercial flight virgin.

5. If you hit turbulence, or worse, think you are about to crash, take comfort in the knowledge that your loved ones will be able to sue the Whale's estate for more than even you ever thought you were worth.

Yachting: Why Really Big Whales Like to Climb on Water

Nothing screams "I am a Whale!" like arriving on your own megayacht. If the yacht's mega enough, what other clubs you do or don't belong to doesn't matter. Drop anchor in any harbor of privilege—Saint Bart's, Nantucket, Newport, Palm Beach,

Sag Harbor, Saint Tropez, Ibiza, the Maldives, etc., in an ocean-going multistoried palace of excess, over three hundred feet in length, and anyone who's anyone on shore is going to know you're someone worth getting to know. Not just because ownership of a half-billion-dollar-plus megayacht indicates that you also possess megabillions, but because you have the balls to flaunt it.

The real pleasure for those Whales fortunate enough to be able to join the megayacht club is the sense of self-confidence and social ease he or she purchases when purchasing a megayacht. When all of those Whales and Big Fish who are stuck on dry land see your crew of forty scurrying around on a deck of your megayacht unloading your toys—speedboats, jet skis, submarine, etc.—and watch you decide which of your two on-board swimming pools to take your morning dip in, they won't simply envy you, they will want to come on board. Hoping you will invite them to your party, they will invite you to their party first, no matter how many bad things they have read about you. A megayacht isn't just a status symbol, it's a letter of recommendation to the world, a passport to whatever fun there is to be had in any given spot on the globe with an ocean breeze.

Yachts have long been a social climbing vehicle of choice for the *très, très, très* riche nouveau-riche Whale. Early in the last century, J. P. Morgan networked the high seas in his 343 feet of ostentatiousness called the *Corsair*. Post Toasties heiress Marjorie Merriwether Post cruised into high society on her football-field-long square rigger, the *Sea Cloud*. It's no wonder

Jackie Kennedy couldn't say no to Greek shipping tycoon and legendary playboy Aristotle Onassis's invitation to come on board—his fabled yacht *Christina O* boasted bar stools upholstered with the foreskin of whales. Who wouldn't want to say they sat on that?

Then and now, size matters to Whales and those who love them. Keeping up this tradition of excess, Microsoft's idea man Paul Allen's yacht, *Octopus*, features the usual swimming pool and helicopter pad, plus a sixty-three-foot tender, seven speedboats, accommodations for twenty-two guests, a recording studio, and not one but two submarines. Launched in 2003 with a length of 414 feet, it was the largest private yacht in the world.

Sadly for Mr. Allen, he lost those bragging rights a year later to Oracle's Larry Ellison's 453-foot *Rising Sun*. Whales being Whales, *Rising Sun* has been eclipsed as the world's largest private yacht by forty-seven-year-old Russian oligarch Roman Abramovich's 533-foot-long *Eclipse*. Which, in addition to having two swimming pools and two helicopter pads, is rumored to have an antimissile defense system and an all-important antipaparazzi shield that automatically fires lasers at intrusive cameras, thus overexposing any unwanted or unflattering snapshots of those on board. For the record, we at *The Social Climber's Bible* are of the opinion this last feature of Abramovich's *Eclipse* is overkill—if your yacht is big and beautiful enough, what you look like in a bathing suit doesn't matter.

Why does size matter so much to Whales? In Mr. Abramovich's case, one would assume he wanted a yacht big enough to house his rumored forty-man security team and to offer him plenty of nooks and crannies to hide in if an uninvited commando team of old friends decide to crash his party. Size also matters simply because it's a thrill to be able to boast to any and all other Whales, "Mine is bigger than yours."

EMPOWERING THOUGHT #51

Of course the size of a Whale's yacht is not directly proportional to the length of his penis, but we do not advise pointing that out to the megayacht-owning Whale if you are hoping to be invited on board.

What every social climber needs to know before boarding a yacht:

1. Do not be surprised if the yacht's owner is not as elegant as his or her vessel.

2. A great guest on board a yacht does not get seasick.

3. Smaller is sometimes better. If you are a guest on a yacht that is more than four hundred feet long, you will run the risk of being moored within spitting distance of a Carnival ocean liner full of tourists, as opposed to being anchored in a picturesque harbor next to topless supermodels or Daniel Craig in a Speedo.

4. If, for instance, the said Whale boat is a classic 134-foot yawl, know that "she" is a sailboat, i.e., there will be no swimming pool, limited room for sunbathing, and the toilets will be smaller than the one you sat on in the private jet you flew in on.

5. When you are a guest on even the biggest of megayachts, you are a captive audience; you are at your Whale's mercy. You go where the Whale goes and do what the Whale wants you to do, except when the megayacht is boarded by pirates or uninvited guests the yacht owner owes large sums of money to. While the Whale is held for ransom, you, no matter how great a guest you are, will be set adrift . . . if you're lucky.

19

CLIMBING THE INNER MOUNTAIN

How do we measure the greatness of a Mountaineer? By the distance climbed, or the highest point achieved during a lifetime. Are Mountaineers only as good as that last rung they were standing on when they met their maker? Do we award style points for technique, superior name-dropping skills, the ability to suck up without ever seeming to be sucking up? Should bonus points be awarded for the number of exclusive clubs a climber has gotten into, or given to those who have successfully married all their children off to Whales without one of them ever signing a prenup? Is the greatest climber the one who made the most money or the one who had the most fun?

Is the most successful climber the one never suspected of being a climber or is it the Mountaineer who got to the top, in spite of the fact that he is an internationally renowned social climber? We say kudos to those reigning size-two society divas touted in glossy magazines who employ PR firms and charm in their assault on the summit for having the courage to climb in public. And more important, we recognize that it took more than their being pushy and having an eating disorder to get where they are today.

How does patriotism figure into the equation used to ascertain greatness? One can become president, prime minister, or a second-rate dictator without being a first-rate patriot, but one cannot be a great politician without being a master social climber. How do we compare their climb to that of the spiritual Mountaineer—the humble parish priest who eventually gets himself elected pope?

> While the question of who is the world's greatest Mountaineer will always be open to debate, one thing is certain: Right now the most important climber in the world to us at *The Social Climber's Bible* is YOU!

We have given you all the basic climbing skills you need to meet and make the kinds of friends who can make your dreams come true. But you have to do your part. Don't just repeat your mantra before you head off to your next cocktail party, wedding, funeral, charity gala, debutante bash, or business meeting. Say "I CARE ENOUGH ABOUT ME NOT TO BELIEVE ANYTHING THEY SAY ABOUT ME IS TRUE IF I DON'T WANT IT TO BE. I WILL NOT BE JUDGED" out loud to yourself each and every morning when you look in the mirror.

Yes, there will be moments of doubt. But if you suddenly feel shy or tongue-tied while trying to impress a Big Fish, just think of Rick James and repeat one of our all-purpose key phrases for polite conversation. Tell them, "They say the same thing about the octopus" in Portuguese and you will be guaranteed a seat in the winner's circle.

Take our advice on how to make the most of Big Fish, Whales, Swans, Turtles, and Unicorns; follow our step-by-step instructions on dating, love, and prenuptials; remember to handwrite thank-you notes; and before you know it, you'll be the kind of person you used to envy.

No one book can contain all there is to know about climbing. You still have a lot to learn. But we promise you, by the time you've mastered the fundamentals outlined on these pages, we will have completed volume two of *The Social Climber's Bible*, and together we'll raise your game to a whole new level.

Great things don't happen by accident. Yes, God has to be on your side, but so do you. The most challenging mountain you must climb lies within yourself: That mountain is called Self-Doubt and is haunted by all those who have snubbed you and have made you think you're unworthy of having your dreams come true. Now that you have read *The Social Climber's Bible*, know this, YOU ARE THE ONLY THING HOLDING YOU BACK FROM MAKING YOUR LIFE GREAT!

Social climbing is about making meaningful friendships each and every day, or as his Holiness, the Dalai Lama, puts it,

> Old friends pass away, new friends appear. It's just like the days.

An old day passes, a new day arrives. The important thing is to make it meaningful: a meaningful friend–or a meaningful day.

Not everyone can be as selfless a Mountaineer as the Dalai Lama, who tirelessly networks and hobnobs with the rich, famous and powerful 24/7/365 for world peace, but you can start making the world a better place by improving your position in it today.

> Stop blaming others for what you don't have, and start making friends who can help you get not just what you want, but what you deserve!

We can't climb the mountain for you, but *The Social Climber's Bible* will be there with you every step of the way. If you run into trouble, need advice about how to impress a Big Fish, get invited to a wedding, or just want to brag about the fabulous week you spent on a Whale's megayacht, email us at popularity@socialclimbersbible.com. For those of you who, after reading our *Bible*, feel inspired to say, "F**k You! Your superficiality makes me embarrassed to be a human being," in advance, we thank you for your opinion, and if you send us your name and address we will do our best to invite you to our next party.

ACKNOWLEDGMENTS

We could not have written *The Social Climber's Bible* without the help of a great many people. Naturally, we would like to acknowledge those individuals who were willing to speak to us openly and honestly about their own personal mountaineering experiences by name . . . but not surprisingly, they preferred to remain anonymous. We would also like to thank those well-known Mountaineers who were eager to meet with us and be quoted on the subject of modern manners but stood us up when they discovered that our title was *The Social Climber's Bible*.

We owe a special debt of gratitude to Patrick Nolan, Emily Murdock Baker, and everyone else at Penguin for their advice, enthusiasm, and most of all, for having the courage to sponsor a serious study of social climbing. And finally, a heartfelt thank-you to our friend and agent, Zoë Pagnamenta, for the encouragement and wise counsel she offered us from day one of this project.